THE
Archive Photographs
SERIES

WIDNES
AND ST HELENS
RAILWAYS

PROUD TO THE END! Waiting to leave St Helens Central on the last day of passenger service in 1952, the footplate staff pose for the photographer.

THE
Archive Photographs
SERIES

WIDNES
AND ST HELENS
RAILWAYS

Compiled by
Bob Pixton

CHALFORD

First published 1996
Copyright © Bob Pixton, 1996

The Chalford Publishing Company
St Mary's Mill, Chalford,
Stroud, Gloucestershire, GL6 8NX

ISBN 0 7524 0751 1

Typesetting and origination by
The Chalford Publishing Company
Printed in Great Britain by
Redwood Books, Trowbridge

Front cover illustration
The famous Runcorn Gap. Trains have been making trips up the line to St Helens
for over 125 years. The dock area is a pleasure area, called Spike Island, with much
of the local track bed under tarmac.

A DAY AT THE RACES. Haydock Park was the successor to nearby Newton race track. This was served by trains from the Haydock Colliery line from the L&M at Earlestown. And we think litter is a modern problem!

Contents

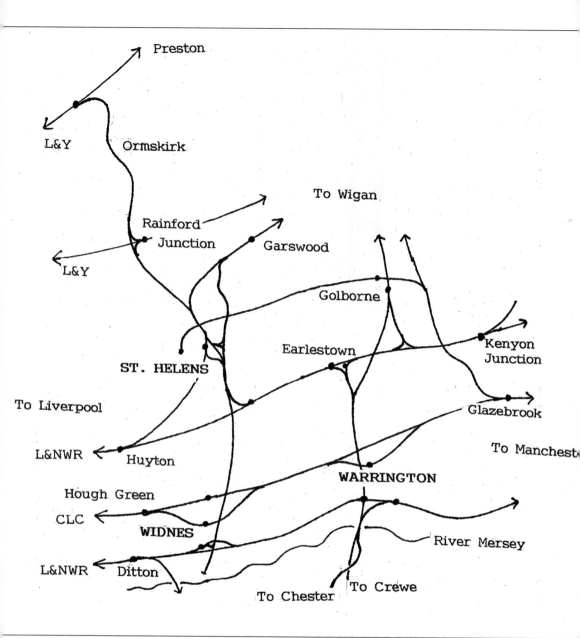

Preston

L&Y

Ormskirk

To Wigan

Rainford
Junction

L&Y

Garswood

Golborne

Kenyon
Junction

Earlestown

ST. HELENS

To Liverpool

Glazebrook

L&NWR   Huyton

To Manchester

Hough Green

WARRINGTON

CLC

River Mersey

WIDNES

L&NWR   Ditton

To Chester   To Crewe

WIDNES/ST HELENS RAILWAY NETWORK, 1922. A view that is no more. While the four almost parallel routes between Lancashire's two largest cities are more or less intact, the majority of the connecting lines have gone. St Helens is only served by the Wigan to Liverpool line and the direct line to Widnes has become part of the road network at both ends.

WIDNES, 1961. While the main line railways dominated the movement of goods between towns, many companies had their own locos for shunting their works. Getting ready to start the day at the ICI factory is 0-4-0T *Wallace*.

Introduction

The railway system around Widnes and St Helens was intimately connected with coal mining and the chemical and glass industries. For about sixty years the owners of the Sankey Brook Navigation had a monopoly on transport in the area. So profitable was the venture, that it paid enormous dividends to the shareholders and, like most such organisations, it neglected its customers.

Deliveries were delayed in winter due to frozen canals and in summer because of lack of water, while the turnpike (toll) roads offered no real alternative. The main movements of freight went down the canal to Runcorn Gap, which we now call Widnes, on to Liverpool, along the River Mersey and down the River Weaver to the salt mining areas of Cheshire. The chief load carried was coal, while in the other direction to St Helens, as well as coal, the canal also supplied the raw materials required by numerous industries.

Hard on the heels of the Liverpool and Manchester Railway came the opening of the St Helens' and Runcorn Gap Railway, officially opened in 1833. Not only did it carry coal from the expanding mines in South Lancashire to St Helens' factories, but sent it down to specially constructed docks adjacent to the locks of the canal at Runcorn Gap. In a move to 'harmonise operations' the canal and railway companies merged: a competitive situation now reverted back to a monopoly!

The extension of the St Helens' line, both east and west from Widnes, was a logical move to transfer goods as near as possible on company metals. However, life in the early 1850s wasn't easy, with bigger companies waiting in the wings ready to capitalise upon economic misfortune, bad management or simply to take over the opposition to safeguard their preferred routes. 'Big Brother', in this case the London and North Western Railway, was ever present. Development of the embryonic Cheshire Lines pushed the western end of the line to beyond its Garston terminus and docks, to Liverpool, in the early 1860s. Soon after, 'Big Brother' really did swallow up the smaller fry. It also opened up a crossing over the River Mersey between Ditton and Runcorn, to Crewe and Chester. Together with the Edge Hill to Garston link, London bound trains were re-routed away from the sharp curve at Earlestown on the L&M, and instead, took this new, faster and shorter line.

Over the next few years, connections from St Helens to Wigan, Rainford, Ormskirk and Huyton, together with expanding coal networks, the chemical industry and glass factories, led to an enormous rail fabric that delivered all things to everyone. In today's car-dominated society the sheer scale is hard to appreciate. Not wanting to dance to anyone else's tune other than their own, the Manchester, Sheffield and Lincolnshire Railway built their own main line from Manchester to Liverpool via Sankey, Farnworth, Widnes and Hough Green.

Not wanting to be dictated to by a single organisation, St Helens' business community put forward the idea of a rival company to link up with the MSLR which had connections not too far away, going north to Wigan. This company, always keen to bury a bone in a rival's back yard, took a wider view and thought of St Helens as a stopping off place for a route to its docks in Liverpool. It would be the start of this century before the line to St Helens opened, and the grandiose scheme to the docks never materialised. As a consequence, one of the earliest casualties of road competition was the passenger service to St Helens' temporary Central Station.

The ever changing face of mining has meant that little coal is now produced in the area and road transport has reduced the freight network to a shadow of its former self. Passenger services, on those lines still open, however, have probably never been as regular, fast or as clean: long may they continue!

SUTTON OAK SHED, 1952. The loco shed for the large number of industrial engines in the St Helens area was south at Sutton. In between duties, probably on a Sunday, is ex-L&Y 0-6-0 ST No. 51397 one of the renowned Barton-Wright rebuild of an Aspinall tender engine.

One

To Widnes from Sankey and Ditton

When passenger services ceased from Liverpool to Manchester by way of Widnes, Warrington and Altrincham, in 1962 that was the end of over 125 years of railway development involving several different railway companies. The first line was from St Helens to Runcorn Gap (Widnes) in 1832, followed by its extension west to Garston in 1852 and east to Warrington, in 1853. The joint LNWR and MSLR line from Manchester's London Road to Broadheath, west of Altrincham was soon followed by part of the Stockport to Warrington line in 1853. All of these came under the 'protective' arm of the LNWR in 1860, and the St Helens' line four years later – the attempt of this company to look after its Liverpool-Manchester line meant that competition had to be absorbed.

WIDNES SOUTH STATION, 1960. Leaving with a typical train of non-corridor coaches is Stanier 2-6-4T No. 42606 in June. This was one of the early morning trains from Liverpool (Lime Street) to Manchester (Oxford Road) via Ditton, Widnes, Warrington and Altrincham. While this section is still in use by coal trains, the station, and most of the buildings have gone: the Widnes by-pass sweeps past the roof of the factory on the left.

SANKEY BRIDGE, 1961. By the time of this eastern view, passenger services had not run since 26 September 1949, twelve years before, although the line had closed for a short period at the end of the First World War, from 1 January 1917 until 1 July 1919. The signal box and the signal protecting the swing bridge were still intact: the latter still exists today, but only as a home arm. The station's facilities were adjacent to the canal and passengers used the sleeper crossing to the signal box to get to the Liverpool platform. The connections to the adjacent Mersey White Lead works look overgrown and out of use; next door, the Sankey Mills also had rail connections.

SANKEY BRIDGES, 1961. This was the scene of an accident in November 1858 involving a train from Kings Cross to Garston. After it crossed the bridge, it was swung to allow canal traffic during the night. Returning as a light engine, the driver missed the stop signal in the fog and ended up in the canal. The MSLR loco *Actaeon* was hauled out several days later, apparently non the worse for wear, and lasted until the 1900s. A west end signal box controlled access to adjacent factories, in addition to this box controlling the swing bridge.

FIDLER'S FERRY (AND PENKETH) 1961. Running parallel to the canal there was a station to serve the isolated community around the lock on the canal. During the construction of the line a kink in the canal was straightened. The suffix was added from April 1881; it reverted to its original name on 3 May 1920. Passengers crossed the line by the footpath and sleeper crossing, the station buildings are to the left. Even though it had not seen passengers since its closure on 2 January 1950, the small adjacent goods yard seems busy. The signal box, like Sankey Bridges, was a standard LNWR brick base with a wooden cabin on top.

FIDLER'S FERRY SIGNAL BOX. In November 1855, the St Helens' Railway directors were pressurised to open a station at Cuerdley, midway between Runcorn Gap and Fidler's ferry, next to the bone works. It wasn't profitable and closed on 5 January 1858. To prevent a repetition, the board placed a level of £3 per week as the minimal income from any future station. When the generating station was built in the early 1960s, the old box was demolished and a new one put up to cope with the access to the loops from the main line. Here, trains arrive from the Arpley and Garston directions.

FIDLER'S FERRY STATION,1959. Common engines on the services from Liverpool were Stanier 2-6-4T sisters Nos. 42606 and 42607. One duty was to work to Warrington (Bank Quay) and then to go via Arpley Junction onto the main line; a service then went back to Lime Street. The deserted and closed, isolated station plays host to the service. The CEGB, and their successors, PowerGen added another 'd' to the name.

CARTERHOUSE JUNCTION, 1984. This signal box is standard LNWR design and its thirty levers control the eastern junction of the original and deviated lines; it is adjacent to Carter's Bridge over the canal and sidings to the Mersey Chemical Works. Its modern function is not only to control traffic along the only line in existence, the deviation, but also to local chemical industries. These, including ACM, used to be accessed from the loop line at Tanhouse Lane but since its closure, this is achieved from a spur nearby, on the deviation.

ORIGINAL LINE. Carterhouse Junction is in the distance in this view from the old footbridge, in which the chemical factory of Albright and Wilson can be seen. Shunting is being done by an industrial saddle tank engine. During the 1850s the railway company increased its tariff for transporting goods and reduced the cost for coal. The embryonic chemical industry in St Helens reasoned that, with few residents on the Mersey marshes, and cheaper costs in Widnes, that was where they would develop and flourish.

ORIGINAL LINE, 1950s. A line side view of part of Albright and Wilsons' chemical factory. The tall signals are for Carterhouse Junction in the east, and behind is Dock Junction. The canal is just visible in the distance. Of interest are the wagons for transporting chemicals. To give some idea of the amounts of coal transported in the early 1860s, 120,000 tons was sent by rail and canal for use in the local industry: twice as much was transported by the canal to the salt works in Cheshire.

ORIGINAL LINE, c. 1961. This was the industrial landscape that was Widnes for 100 years: tall chimneys and mounds of chemicals. Looking across the Warrington-Garston line is the canal with sidings full of wagons on Spike Island. Just visible is the viaduct taking the line from Ditton Junction to Runcorn.

FLAT CROSSING AT WIDNES, 1967. One of the biggest operating problems on the line was this crossing. This is where the 1832 north-south line from St Helens to Widnes is crossed by the 1853 east-west line. Action was called for, and in 1870 it was proposed to build a loop north of the existing line that would go up from the east, over the St Helens' line. To the west, the elevated line would come back down to meet the original line. In doing so the railways of Widnes became complicated. Viewed from the footbridge on 5 August, Standard Class 4 2-6-0 No. 76077 is passing east with an enthusiast's special.

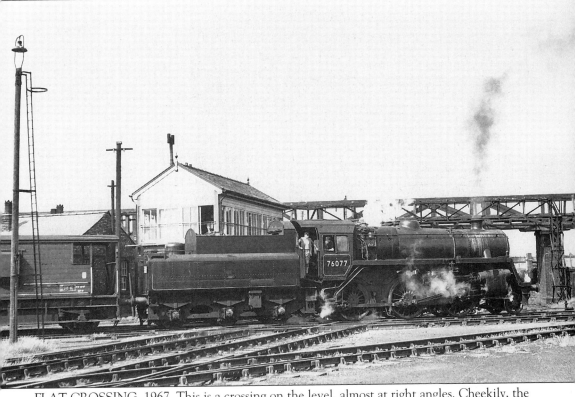

FLAT CROSSING, 1967. This is a crossing on the level, almost at right angles. Cheekily, the builder put in a north-west curve that wasn't in the permission, but was allowed to retain it. Later the east-south curve in the foreground was built. Dock Junction box used to be on the east of the line until this box was built in 1894. Typical of the Widnes scene are the gantries carrying pipes between various buildings belonging to the numerous chemical manufacturers. Controlling the dangerous flat crossing was box No. 4; its fifty-four levers also looked after the curves that allowed north-west and east-south movements.

Standard class engines were born from the need to have locomotives which required the minimum of attention and did well on all grades of fuel. The engines also had to go greater distances between services and had to be easy to maintain and repair.

Generally, they were no more powerful than their 'Big Four' counterparts. However, it was the first time in the country that engineers had had the opportunity to start a new design and incorporate the best practices of different locomotives.

One of the visible trademarks of them is the high running plate. This was because a key principle in the design was that every part which might need attention should be readily accessible: previously, often appearance rather than maintaince, dictated design. Thus, standard class engines are not usually regarded as 'elegant', more 'workman-like'.

WATERLOO ROAD CROSSING. On the extreme left is the deviation line on a bridge; Widnes, LNWR Station buildings are in the recess, the big structure was the baths. The original line crossed the Waterloo Road, controlled by No. 6 box. Widnes' second station was to the west. It superseded the 1832 single platform which had stood adjacent to the canal on the line from St Helens for twenty-one years, but had an even shorter shelf life, succumbing to the station on the deviation some seventeen years later.

26 L. & N.W.	LIVERPOOL, WIDNES, WARRINGTON and MANCHESTER.														Sundays		
	A.M.	A.M.	A.M.	A.M.	A.M.	P.M.	P.M.	P.M.	P.M.	P.M.	P.M.	P.M.	P.M.	P.M	A.M.	P.M.	P.M.
Liverpool (Lime-st) ... dep	6 10	8 5	8 15	9 5	9 55		12	25	1 15		2 45	3 35	4 20	5 10	1055	7 35	10 7 15
Edgehill	6 15	8 10		9 10	10 10		12	30	1 20		2 50	3 40	4 25	5 15	1055	7 40	10 20
Wavertree	6 20	8 14		9 14	10 4		12	18	1 24		2 54			5 20 6 15		11 4	7 45 8 2
Sefton Park	6 22	8 16		9 5	10 6		12	20	1 20		2 56	4 31	5 22 6 17		11 6		
Mossley Hill	6 25	8 19		9 18	10 9		12	35	1 23		2 59	4 35	5 25 6 20		11 10		
Allerton	6 29	8 23		9 22	10 13		12	39	1 34		3 3	4 38	5 30 6 24		1115		
Speke	6 34	8 27			10 17				1 40		3 7	4 42	5 34 6 28			8 0	12 3 7 40
Halebank	6 40	8 31			10 21		12	46	1 46		3 12	4 47	5 39 6 34			8 6	2 41 7 46
Ditton Junction	6 46	8 41		9 31	10 35		12	52	1 52		3 16	4 51	5 51 6 45		1126	8 10	2 46 7 50
Widnes ... arr	7 0	8 48	8 30	9 34	10 39	1155	12	55	2 2		3 20	3 58	4 55 5 50 6 53	7 48	11 3	8 14	2 50 7 54 11 3
Fiddler's Ferry	7 9	8 54		9 42	10 45	12 5			2 11		3 27		4 6 5 6 58	STOP 9 19	STOP	8 22	8 57 8 2
Sankey Bridges	7 13			9 45		12 7			2 15		3 31		5 6 6 7	9 23		8 26	1 8 6
Warrington (B'nk Qy)	7 16	8 58		9 48	10 51	1210	1	8	2 18		3 34	4 7	5 16 6 97	9 26	1112	8 29	3 4 8 9
,, Arpley ... dep	7 17	9 0		9 55	10 53	1253	1	11	2 20		3 35	4 9	5 16 10 7	9 30	1140	8 46	5 8 10
Latchford	7 19	9 2		9 58	10 57	1256	1	18	2 25		3 38	4 11	5 22 6	9 32		8 50	8 8 12
Lymm	7 25	9 7		10 2	11 2	1240	1	18	2 27		3 42	4 15	5 22 6	9 37		8 55	12 8 18
Broadheath (Altrincham)	7 35	9 15		1010	11 11	1248	1	28	2 35		3 50	4 24	5 30 6 28 7 40	9 45	1150	9 5	20 8 28
Stockport	7 50	9 27		1025	11 26	1 3	1	41	2 49		4 4	4 30	5 43 6 44 7 54			9 19	5 34 8 44
Macclesfield	8 37				11 54		2	6				4 50	6 5 7 13 8 23		1215		
Manchester (Lond-rd) ...	8 42				12 43		3	3				5 51	6 41 8 30 29				1215
	8 15	9 47		1048	11 55		2	53	10		4 30	5 20	6 57 7 8 8 24		1230	9 50	4 5 9 15 1230

Manchester (Lond-rd) dep			7 5		7	50	9 20		10 25		1230	2 0	2 55		3 40	5 20	6 55	9 5		7 36	1 40 6 30
Macclesfield					7	50	8 35				1139				2 5		6 15				
Stockport			7 5		8	15	9 13				12 7				3 32		6 40				
Broadheath (Altrincham)			7 35		9	0	9 42		10 49		1252	1 24	2 33		3 40	5 46	7 16	9 29		8 0	2 10 7 0
Lymm			7 48		9	14	9 52		11		1 9	1 37	2 50		4 18	6 1	7 31	9 45		8 15	2 25 7 15
Latchford			7 55		9	22	10 0		11 11		1 20	1 45	3 0	3 38	4 26	6 9	7 39	9 54		8 23	3 37 23
Warrington Arpley ...			7 58		9	25	10 4		11 14		1 24	1 49	3 4	3 41	4 29	6 12	7 42	9 57		8 27	2 36 7 26
,, (B'nk Qy) arr			8 2		9	28	10 7		11 18		1 29	1 53	3 8	3 44	4 32	6 18	7 45	10 0		8 29	3 47 7 30
,, dep	7 27	8 23		9	45	10 9		11 55		1 55	3 20	3 47		5 15	6 20		8	9 5	2 40 8 0
Sankey Bridges	7 31	8 28		9	50			11 57		2 15	3 24	3 51		5 19	6 24		4	9 12	44 8 4
Fiddler's Ferry	7 35	8 32		9	54			12 1		2 3	3 28	3 55		5 25	6 28		8 1010	9 13	48 8 8
Widnes	6 0	7 40	8 40	9 3	10	5	10 18	1024	12 8	1 30	2 15	3 35	4 0 5	7 5	134 6 35	7 20 8 13	1023	1114	8 69	2 1 2 56 8 14
Ditton Junction	6 5	8 0	8 45	9 26	10	8		1032	12 13	1 34	2 20	3 41	5	5 38	6 48 7 5	8 1030	1136	9 10	2 53 1 8 21
Halebank			8 4	8 48		stop			10 24			2 25		5 42	6 52	7 43 8 23	1034		9 24	5 1 8 31
Speke			8 10				12 19	1 46		2 30		5 48	6 58	7 49 8 29			9 36	1 8 34
Allerton	6 14	8 15	8 56	9 35	10	33	1041	12 24	1 46	2 32	3 50		5 53	7 3	7 54 8 1041	1043		9 40	5 10 8 36
Mossley Hill	6 19	8 20	9 0	9 39	10	37	11a14	12 28	1 50	3 54		5 18	5 58	7	7 59 8 1049			9 45	5 21 8 41
Sefton Park	6 22	8 23	9 3	9 17	9 42		11a17		2 a 0	3 12		4 35		5 21	6 2	7 10 8 28 42 1018			
Wavertree	6 25	8 25	8a19	9 45			11a19	1 a 0	1 65	3 14	4a38		5 23	6 4	7 13 8 4 8 4651			9 50	5 26 8 46
Edgehill	6 29	8 29	9 7	9 45			10 45	1050	12 35	1 a 0	2 39	4 2		5 26	6 8	7 17 8 8 49 1055	1750	9 28	9 55 30 8 50
Liverpool (Lime-st) ... arr	6 35	8 35	9 12	9 50			10 48	1055	12 40	1 61		4 8		5 31	6 15	7 25 8 15 8 55 1050 1750		9 35	10 0 3 35 8 55

* Sat. only.   § Sat. excep.   ‡ Arrive 5-28   Y—Calls to set down on notice being given
a Change at Allerton.   b Arrives 6-49   Saturdays arrive 7-3   c Saturdays arrive 7-3

●—Cheap Bookings: Widnes to Liverpool—Monday, Thursday and Saturday; returning same day after 5 p.m.
Widnes to Manchester—Monday, Thursday and Saturday; returning same day after 6 p.m.

TIMETABLE FOR 1908.

WATERLOO CROSSING, 1961. Romantic they may be to some, but a nuisance to all the travelling public they definitely were. A small tank engine shunts wagons in March causing everyone to wait: even the van from whose window this view was taken! As there was no footbridge, pedestrians also had to wait. All trace of this crossing, and the lines on both sides have been swept away but the station buildings still exist. Just south of the current railway bridge, to the east and recessed from the road, is a white-fronted storage building.

WIDNES, DEVIATION LINE. Passing east along the elevated lines with a train of coal empties is a BR Standard Class 2-10-0. The lines adjacent to the shed connect the original St Helens line to the Widnes-Warrington line. Behind them, rising at a gradient of 1 in 60 to the left, is the curve from the original line up to meet the deviation at Widnes Station. There used to be a very long footbridge passing the canal and railway lines to Anne Street.

WIDNES, LNWR STATION, 1957. To cope with the new deviation line, the second (1853) passenger station to the west of the Waterloo Crossing, closed. This new one opened above the roof tops of Widnes on 1 March 1870. The booking office was at street level and steps led up to the platforms, adjacent to the white sheds. The signal box is Widnes No. 7, with its twenty levers. When the deviation was built, a spur was also put in to link it with the St Helens' line it passed over, allowing passenger trains from St Helens to use the new station. The solid looking LNWR semaphore signals belie the presence of the spur.

EX-WIDNES SOUTH 1976. This view to the west shows the gradient the trains had to climb on the deviation line after it was closed to passengers, but still very much open to freight traffic. The point work for the spur down to the St Helens' line is immediately in front of the photographer, the pre-grouping signals finally making way for BR style ones. When the nearby ex-MSLR and MR station closed, this station became 'South' on 1 May 1959 to distinguish it from 'North' on the CLC main line. It eventually closed on 10 September 1962. Apart from the removal of the junction, the signal box and the platforms, this is the view today.

HUTCHINSON STREET GOODS YARD. The goods yard is served by the lines off to the right. The shunter's line, and the one next to it, are the original lines from Warrington to Ditton with the deviation line going up to the left. Victoria Road is in the distance.

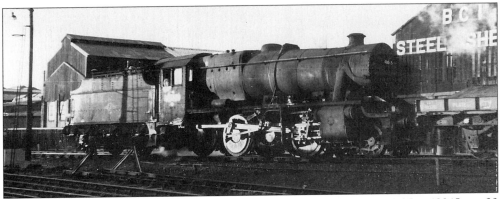

DEVIATION LINE, 1963. Coming down the slope is Stanier 8F 2-8-0 No. 48045 on 23 November. The background factory belongs to Burning Corrugated Iron. Close to the separation of the Runcorn and Widnes lines the British Oxygen Co. had rail access from 1971 to early 1990s. Trains went to Wembley, Sheffield and Wolverhampton; one block train of ten wagons was equivalent to thirty of the largest road tankers of the day.

DE SOTO BRIDGE. Threading its way from the slow lines to those that will enable the train to pass along the deviation, is a train of coal empties from Garston docks. The signal box, West Deviation, was rebuilt in the early 1970s, in the same style as Fiddler's Ferry. On the left can be made out the parapet of the Marsh Branch from the MSLR and MR line to the West Bank docks.

WIDNES WEST DEVIATION BOX, 1976. This was the point where the deviation came down to meet the original Widnes-Garston line. The bridge is Marsh Road. Originally the box had fifty levers; the 1956 rebuild had thirty-six.

DITTON, 1959. Over one hundred years before, the St Helens' Railway extended east to better docks at Garston, opening on 1 July 1852. It was possible, with omnibus connections to the city of Liverpool, Castle Street, to get to London on GNR trains. What had been lines designed for freight now were increasingly catering for passengers. From 15 February 1864, the LNWR ran trains from Lime Street on its new line via Edge Hill, to Garston and Warrington. The St Helens' Railway Company's prize of an access to Liverpool was achieved at last. Five years later the LNWR opened the line across the Mersey by the Runcorn Bridge. This meant that the main route south ceased to be along the L&M to Earlestown, and then via Warrington, but was now south via Ditton, Runcorn and Crewe. This new line rose up and passed over the original line. This made Ditton an extremely busy part of the St Helens' Railway. The original station closed and a new one, some 250 yards west, opened on 1 May 1871, just west of the Hale Road. This became the western terminus for the St Helens' trains and for many from Manchester. Connections on the Liverpool-Chester service enabled people to get to the city from a variety of places. In December, Royal Scot 4-6-0 No. 46124 *London Scottish* emerges from under the Hale Road Bridge with a Liverpool to Llandudno train.

DITTON, c. 1905. This view looks west to the station, with its buildings perched on top of the Hale Road Bridge. The three sets of signals control, from the right, the Warrington North line, the Crewe line and the Warrington South line. The controlling box is No. 1. Hoops on arms was a LNWR device to indicate 'goods', or 'slow' lines, it was phased out after the grouping. Just visible to the right of the station buildings are the even taller posts for the up direction. Ditton Station's platforms can be seen under the bridge.

DITTON JUNCTION CRASH, 1912. A Liverpool destined train (the 5.30 from Chester) of two horse boxes and seven coaches had just descended the 1 in 114 from Runcorn Bridge, hauled by Precedent 2-4-0 No. 1529 *Cook*, and was approaching Ditton on the middle set of lines at about 60 mph. The signal post in front of it showed that the middle set of signals were off. This, in practise, meant that the train was to transfer from the fast to slow lines by the second crossover; the right hand signals were the down fast straight on indicators. A crash ensued. This shot shows the tender being put onto a low loader aided by an army of on-lookers, which contemporary newspapers reported, hampered the rescue work.

DITTON JUNCTION CRASH, 1912. Due to lack of knowledge of the road, the engine didn't slow down and was consequently derailed at the crossover. The engine slid on its side up to the brick work of the bridge and the boiler and boiler became detached from the chassis. The leading horse box was hurled clean over the bridge to land on the platforms: the startled horse escaped unhurt. The train crew died as did all the passengers in the first two coaches. As the coaches were gas-lit, it was lucky that none were burned to death although fire did break out. The parts are being loaded onto low loaders in this 'posed' shot. The firebox and boiler are being lifted by a steam crane while the chassis is to the left.

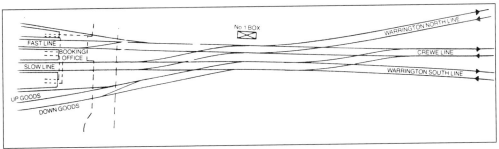

DITTON JUNCTION, 1912.

DITTON JUNCTION, 1936. Since the accident things have changed. A new No. 1 box is now on the opposite side of the line and there is only one crossover, at a gentler angle, between the lines. A creosoting works has been developed to the north of the line. Passing the signal box is a Class 5 4-6-0 with a mixture of coaches and an up express.

DITTON JUNCTION, 1957. It is just after 5.30 on 10 April and arriving with the 4.05 from Manchester (London Road), is Stanier 2-6-4T No. 42607. The all stations to Liverpool's Lime Street would arrive at 6.10. The massive, tall LNWR signal posts were being dismantled with their arms on smaller, lower posts.

DITTON, 1960. Twenty-five year old Crewe built Class Five 4-6-0 No. 45074 is passing east with a train of meat containers in August along the up slow. Old No. 2 signal box is in the background on the left; soon it will be demolished with its functions taken over by the new box on the right.

DITTON JUNCTION, 1962. The station was completely rebuilt for the electrification of the line from Liverpool to Crewe in the early 1960s. Stanier 2-6-2T No. 41211 has arrived with the 4.19 from Manchester's Oxford Road. A report in *Railway Magazine* in May 1961 showed that the same train, hauled by Standard 84001, had only nineteen passengers with no one using it at six of the intermediate stations. While the evening and morning services were well patronised, it would be hard to see any great savings that could be made due to the large number of level crossings that would need to be manned due to the number of freight trains. Such evidence was ignored when the withdrawal of train services was contemplated.

DITTON, 1961. This view under the new road bridge in March shows the pre-stressed reinforced concrete footbridge. The station buildings on top of the road bridge may have been appropriate for a less mobile society, but in today's car dominated society they are a liability, especially as there is also a sharp bend. The new No. 1 box can be made out under the overhead wire clutter. The routes east are to Crewe, flanked by Warrington's north and south. It is along the latter that Stanier 8F 2-8-0 No. 48722 sets its train back along.

DITTON JUNCTION NO. 1 BOX, 1984. When the line was electrified in 1961, the whole area was rebuilt: the station, the Hale Road Bridge and to control events, this new signal box. Inter City expresses and Liverpool-Crewe local trains ignore the new station, with only a few rush hour trains stopping there. Were the transport planners right to optimistically rebuild the station when one looks at the congestion in South Lancashire? What would the local scene be like if the route was still available for through passenger traffic? The station closed on 27 May 1994.

Two
To Widnes Central from Sankey and Hough Green

This part of the line, from Sankey to Hough Green, opened to passengers on 1 August 1873, five months after goods trains had first used it. The line was part of the Cheshire Lines Committee's desire for an independent line from Manchester to Liverpool. Until then, their trains had to pass on lines that operated jointly or which belonged to rivals.

WIDNES CENTRAL STATION, 1964. An Ivatt Flying Pig 2-6-0, probably No. 43013, departs from MRLR and MR joint station with the last train: the 4.56 to Manchester Central on 5 October. Four minutes earlier, a two car DMU left with the last westbound train for Liverpool Central.

SANKEY (FOR PENKETH) STATION, 1961. A mile distant from Warrington Station where the avoiding line joins from the right at Sankey Junction, crosses the St Helens' canal and after another mile and a half, reaches Sankey Station. From August 1939, sidings were laid for the RAF maintenance unit at Burtonwood; it also served as a wartime base for the USAF. They closed at the end of the war and for a short time after 1976, were re-opened. This view looks west, showing the typical CLC station buildings on the Liverpool, down, platform with a shelter on the other platform.

SANKEY STATION SIGNAL BOX. This was situated at the western end of the Manchester platform. Its duty, apart from controlling the section between Sankey Junction (to the east) and Widnes East (to the west), was to control the loop and small goods yard on the down side.

SIGNALS AT SANKEY, 1961. Sight lines over bridges presented opportunities for signalling engineers to show how they could communicate with foot plate crews at a distance commensurate with the speeds desired. Curves in the line made things difficult at times. Sankey had its share of unique signals. West of the station there was a tall post just by the bridge visible in the previous view. It had an upper up arm (to Manchester) at the top with a lower down starter arm, just visible above the bridge. This signal post was on the Manchester side of the bridge from which the above photograph was taken. It shows the up starter, which would be visible from a train in the station, with its repeater arm hoisted up high so that it would be visible some way off by trains not stopping at the station. Due to the bend in the line (and also as an economy measure!) the down starter signal is on the same post; to aid sighting it too is skywards. Coloured lights don't have the same appeal.

WIDNES NORTH, 1961 (above), 1976 (below). Yet another CLC clone station: buildings on the Liverpool platform have a fancy bargeboard and there is a shelter for Manchester passengers. Both platforms were independently accessed from the adjacent over bridge. With the closure of the goods yard in 1964 and the resignalling, the area to the west has been razed to the ground. Access to the platforms now is via the main buildings or from a narrow pathway at the end of the Manchester bound platform, with a footbridge connecting them. Unlike most stations on the line, the CLC style shelter has been replaced by a steel and glass bus stop type. After the closure of Widnes Central, this station became the 'North' station on 5 January 1959 to differentiate it from the ex-LNWR station that was called 'South'. When that closed to passengers, this station lost its suffix completely on 5 May 1968.

FARNWORTH, c. 1910. Unmistakably CLC, the station buildings are identical to many on the Liverpool-Manchester main line. Racing through it, at what seemed like an incredible 'mile a minute' is GCR single No. 972. The six of this class were obsolete before they were operational, consequently Robinson cancelled the remaining four. Intended for the London Extension, they were under powered for the job so were farmed out to lighter, easier graded lines like the CLC. The livery was Brunswick Green and Crimson Lake. With a reduction in their boiler pressure from 200 to 160 lbs per square inch, their lives were extended: 972 lasted until August 1927. The fast services between the cities of Manchester and Liverpool were timed to leave both termini at the same time, '30 minutes past the hour', which was a good publicity exercise.

At the time of this photograph the service to Farnworth was sparse, with more trains going round to Widnes Central and by-passing here. After nationalisation the situation had not only reversed, but the '30 minutes past the hour' trains from both termini stopped here. This gave the residents of Widnes, for the first time, access to speedy trains to Liverpool and Manchester as well as daily trains to Nottingham and Hull.

FARNWORTH TUNNEL. The line between Lancashire's two principal cities was a switch back affair due to the up and down nature of the terrain. East of Farnworth was a short (100 yards), shallow (less than 20 feet) tunnel. On top was a canvas works and its associated lakes. It was opened out in the 1920s making today's deep cutting.

FARNSWORTH CUTTING. The opening out of the tunnel has moved on a stage. The brickwork forming the roof and portals has been removed and a small retaining wall has been built. The surrounding rock is being removed into rail wagons and onto the contractor's own narrow gauge lines, aided by a steam crane. The signal gantry is interesting.

HOUGH GREEN, 1947. This station opened some sixteen months after the line, just after Liverpool Central admitted passengers, in May 1874. In common with many others, the station buildings are identical. This view, east, is towards Manchester and it shows the line off to the left that leads to Widnes. Note the ownership on the hoarding on the left, the station's name on the seat of the Liverpool platform and the gas lamps spaced out along the wall.

HOUGH GREEN, 1963. Another shot from the road bridge, looking east, but this time at the limited facilities on the Manchester platform. Apart from coloured lights, electric lamps and a lick of paint, little has changed between the previous view and this. Today, part of the Widnes loop is now a road and such a view would include many more houses and far less countryside. Although Ditton was some distance away, Hough Green had been 'for Ditton' since at least just after the turn of the century. The loco Stanier 2-6-4T No. 42612 would be on its way to Warrington as the passenger services had become the monopoly of DMUs, as the stopping indicator on the platform shows.

WIDNES (NORTH), 1964. Britannia Pacific No. 70050 *Firth of Clyde* waits for shunting instructions. It has gone onto the 'wrong line' in readiness to go into the goods yard. Behind it are carflats from Longbridge, Birmingham, with new Austin Healey cars. A local car dealer had leased the redundant yard as a distribution centre. This engine was built ten years earlier, at Crewe and was originally allocated to the Scottish region, hence the name. Britannias were built in two batches, this was one of the ten in the second lot, with modifications in the light of experiences from the first batch.

Alterations visible here are the single foot plate beneath the smoke box, a grab rail on the tender, the latter being type BR10. This differed by having flush sides with a high curved top replacing the inset coal space. Internally it carried 2 tons more coal and almost 500 gallons more water.

TANHOUSE LANE STATION, 1961. When the CLC line was planned near Widnes in the early 1870s, the local people applied pressure, as at Warrington, for the line to loop through the town rather than to avoid it. This stemmed from the LNWR's insistence that factories connect to the north-south line rather than to the better connected, east-west line. Plans were approved in 1873 for the Widnes Railway to run for approximately three miles from east and west triangular connections with the main line at Barrows Green, to a point close to Anne Street; this was still east of the LNWR line. The next year the GNR objected to this line being absorbed by the CLC, and so it became an MSLR and MR line, opening for goods on 3 April 1877.

Tanhouse Lane Station was a later addition to this freight first network on 1 September 1890. As can be seen from this western view, it consisted of up and down platforms with facilities on both. They were connected by a footbridge which doubled as a public crossing over the line when the adjacent level crossing was in use.

TANHOUSE LANE STATION. In 1874 local landowners re-submitted plans for the Widnes (West) Junction Railway. This was to have east and west connections with the CLC near Hough Green and would be about two miles long. Along its length it would serve local industries ending at the Ditton Iron Works on the banks of the River Mersey. At the same time an extension to the above former Widnes Railway was proposed. This would link it up with the Widnes (West) Junction Railway giving a loop through the town. The central and western parts opened on 1 July 1879, having extensive connections with Hutchinson's West Bank estates at Moor Lane Junction. Alterations went on continually right up to its closure. The signal had the small bracket added in the late 1950s when the name board was replaced and the station was painted.

TANHOUSE LANE STATION, 1955. Arriving from the Manchester direction is Black Five 4-6-0 No. 45201. On the right is part of Mersey Chemical works. Raising of freight charges to St Helens in the 1870s and the opportunity to move to the uninhabited marshy banks of the River Mersey led to the transfer of many prosperous chemical industries from St Helens to Widnes. With only nine trains each way per day in 1951 and the onslaught from cars about to begin, the station closed on 5 October 1964.

TANHOUSE LANE SHED, 1951. This is looking east to the level crossing that gave the station its name. Next to it is the controlling signal box and the fine, tall stop signal post. The CLC developed this two road shed in the late 1890s. The perennial problem with this and other sheds was always the roof. The southern set of smoke vents is in a poor state, in three years time it was removed like the wooden doors which have already gone. Note the water column. Inside, on 10 November, was LNER Class J10 No. 68547, typical of the sort of engine needed to shunt the numerous connections to industries.

TANHOUSE LANE, 1964. Storming out of the yard is 9F 2-10-0 No. 92019. The new ballast on its line is because this chord has not long been opened. It joined the LNWR system, by No. 1 box, to the MSLR and MR joint loop. This allowed the rest of the joint line to be closed. The engine is hauling empty hoppers back to Long Meg where they will be refilled and sent south. Despite the closure of many lines, these were profitable lines and kept open. When the United Sulphuric Acid Corporation plant closed in the early 1970s, a link was put in from the LNWR line at Carterhouse Junction to Tanhouse yard. Consequently, the line north of St Helens closed. The two trains each weekday in 1955 were timed to leave Long Meg at 9 am and 2.55 pm, initially both following the same route to Blackburn. There, the earlier train went via Lostock Hall and Ormskirk to get onto the ex-CLC system at Aintree. The later train gained the CLC system via the Whelley loop around Wigan and then the GC line from there to Stagebrook. Closure of lines around Wigan and Liverpool meant that later these trains were sent along the former LU line from Wigan to St Helens and then fown to Widnes.

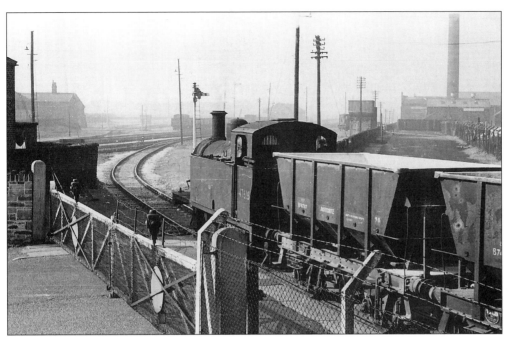

TANHOUSE LANE, 1963. Shunting wagons into the USAC plant at Tanhouse Lane is 0-6-0T No. 47616. Two daily trains each way, brought anhydrite from Long Meg, near Settle. This was a two day journey. One train stabled overnight at Walton-on-the-Hill and approached from the west. The other went via Wigan and the LNWR line from St Helens.

HALE ROAD TUNNEL, 1922. The line from Widnes Central to Hough Green went into a short tunnel as it went under the Liverpool Road. On the left is the primary school that is still there today, although not as a school, while the houses make up Elizabeth Terrace.

41

WIDNES CENTRAL STATION. Opening on 1 August 1879, this station was up on a viaduct, not fifty metres north of the LNWR station on their deviated line which had opened nine years earlier. Widnes Central Station closed on 5 October 1964. This view east, two years before closure, shows a deserted station: there was no service on Sundays.

WIDNES CENTRAL STATION, STAFF PHOTOGRAPH. Looking rather like a football team, this 'posed' shot of staff shows the high level of employment the railways had in pre-grouping days. The station master would have had ticket collectors, porters and parcelmen as well as signalmen and shunting staff under him. Waiting, on the wrong line, is GCR loco No. 864.

Three
Widnes to St Helens via Clock Face and Sutton

This line was one of the country's oldest lines and was conceived as a means to convey coal to the city of Liverpool and the salt mining areas on the River Weaver in Cheshire. Previously this traffic had been the monopoly of the Sankey Brook Navigation.

WIDNES DOCK CROSSING, 1960. Austerity 2-8-0 No. 90054 is hauling a mixed freight train for St Helens in September. The middle of the train is crossing the Sankey Canal on the 1833 swing bridge. On the horizon are the Runcorn Transporter Bridge and its replacement, a fixed road bridge still under construction.

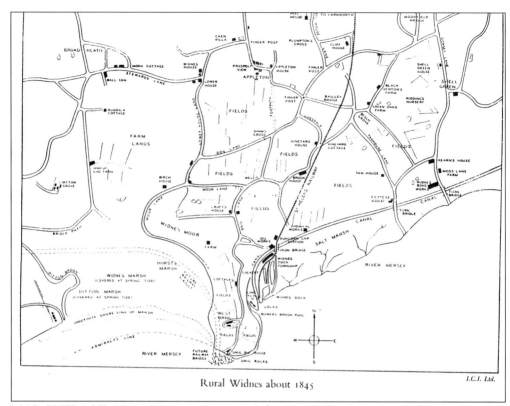

Rural Widnes about 1845

I.C.I. Ltd.

MAP EXTRACT 1845. (From *A History of the Chemical Industry in Widnes* by Hardie.)

The St Helens' Railway was born out of the desire to break the monopoly on transporting coal by canal from St Helens to the River Mersey and hence to Liverpool and the salt producing areas of Cheshire around the River Weaver. A canal, the Sankey Brook Navigation, was developed in 1757 to open into the Sankey Brook to the east of Warrington; this emptied into the tidal River Mersey. Five years after opening the canal was extended two miles to the east to open directly into the Mersey by a lock at Fidler's Ferry. These were prosperous times for shareholders: not only was a dividend of 33 per cent paid, but the market value of the shares was eight times their nominal value. Like all monopolies, it is easy to become complacent. The canal owners made minimal effort to be effective: delays in winter caused by frozen water and in summer due to insufficient water, were frequent but unremedied. So confident were the owners that no other form of transport could challenge them. However, the threat of the railway was taken seriously and the company extended the canal again, just over two miles to Widnes, where they had built twin locks of 79 ft by 20 ft which opened into the Mersey. The line officially opened on 22 February 1833, after carrying coal trains for a few months since the previous November. The docks opened on Spike Island later, on 26 July. The position was such that amalgamation between the two was proposed and from 21 July 1845, the St Helens' Canal and Railway was formed, creating a virtual monopoly. It is easy, historically, to paint the picture that canals were eclipsed as soon as railways appeared. In fact it wasn't until the early 1850s that the line carried more than the canal: often the profitable canal bailed out the bankrupt railway.

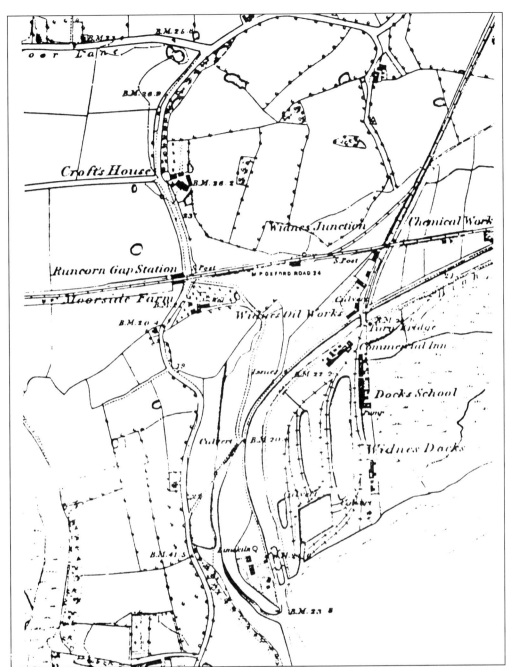

SIX INCH: MILE MAP OF RUNCORN GAP. There were, however, problems associated with the docks and locks at Runcorn Gap. They were inaccessible for eighty days a year which led the company to look to the west, to deep water docks at Garston. An extension to Warrington in the east meant that the company had two separate systems that crossed almost at a right angle, at Runcorn Gap. An unsanctioned north-west tight curve joined the two systems. Officially, on 1 July 1853, a new Runcorn Gap Station was opened on the east-west line, west of the Waterloo Road level crossing, with the original station closing. The name Widnes only came into being from 1 September 1864.

WIDNES SOUTH STATION. Due to the operational problems caused by the flat crossing, a northern elevated loop was built. This went from Carterhouse Junction, in the east, up and over the St Helens' line, and then down to meet the original line at West Deviation near Marsh Road. A third station was opened on the elevated line by the Waterloo Road Bridge, less than 100 yards north of the second station, on 1 March 1870. This view looks west, showing a Stanier 8F 2-8-0 hauling a freight train up the 1 in 120 along the deviation line.

WIDNES SOUTH STATION, 1957. Waiting to go down the 1 in 60 spur from the deviation to meet the original north-south line, is Standard Class 2-6-0 No. 78039. It is probably on its way to the engine shed. Widnes No. 7 box controls events. As this was made up ground, the LNWR's policy for signal boxes was that they should be of lightweight construction, hence the all wood building.

WIDNES SHED, 1931. LNWR 'G' Class 0-8-0 engine No. 9169 adds to the smoky atmosphere outside the shed. Stanier 2-8-0s replaced them and soon after this photograph the northlight roof was replaced. In the background is part of the long footbridge that went from the narrow passage in Croft Street, opposite Alforde Street, across the line to the canal.

WIDNES LOCO SHED, 1961. A two road shed was built in 1874 on a cramped site between the elevated line and the spur down to meet the St Helens' line. It was enlarged in 1881 as a typical six road building. In view is Standard 2-6-0 No. 78035 and poking its nose out of the shed is an 8F 2-8-0. Stanier 2-6-2Ts Nos. 41244 and 41248 would be used on passenger services to St Helens or Manchester, both of which tended to start at Ditton Junction. The line to the right led to the coal, water and the turntable facilities, access to the latter involves a reversal.

WIDNES LOCO SHED TURNTABLE, 1955. It was officially code 8D under LMS/BR, with the parent shed being Edge Hill. Unusually, when the MSLR and MR shed at Tanhouse Lane closed, its allocation was sent to Widnes for stabling, although maintained by Brunswick. One such engine was this ex-LNER J10/4 0-6-0 No. 65157. Due to the cramped nature of the site, the 42 ft turntable was close to the entrance to the shed while the coal and water were to the side of the shed, thus servicing wasn't a straight 'cafeteria' affair.

WIDNES YARD, 1962. Looking north from the footbridge, this view gives a good idea of the cramped position of the yard. In the background is the elevated deviated line. The water tower, coal hole and shed are sandwiched between it and the lines rising up from left to right which will meet the deviation at No. 7 box. Tank engine No. 41230 is in steam by the shed, while sister engine No. 40143 is dumped in the sidings. The original line is in front of this engine, with the flat crossing on the left.

WIDNES LOCO SHED YARD, 1963. Looking north across the shed yard on 12 October, the elevated line can be seen in the background. The Ivatt Mogul 2-6-0 No. 46424 was a lightweight version of the well-known Hughes-Fowler Crabs and the less numerous Stanier Class. As mixed traffic engines they were well suited to the variety of tasks that they would have to perform towards the end of steam, ranging from shunting, freight trips and passenger turns. Note the cab protection afforded from the tender. Many were built with double chimneys and had poor steaming records, so they were re-built with better performing single chimneys.

INTERIOR, WIDNES LOCO SHED, 1955. Due to frequent sharp bends in the numerous industrial concerns in the area, short wheel base engines were necessary. On 28 August ex-L&Y 0-4-0 ST Pug No. 51204 was inside the shed. It was built just after the turn of the century for the L&Y as No. 1156, becoming LMS No. 11204, and saw service in many of the Liverpool docks. In 1946 the northlight roof was replaced by the LMS louvre style.

ANNE STREET, 1967. After skirting the loco depot, the spur down from the east-west line joins the original north-south line from St Helens to the docks. On 1 August, Stanier 8F 2-8-0 No. 48296 is about to go under the deviated line and pass the junction with the spur. The points look set for straight on and so the train of mineral wagons is bound for the industries to the south of Widnes, or across the canal to the docks onto what is now called Spike Island. The bridge was the whole reason for the deviation, making it possible to cross the St Helens line without causing an obstruction.

WIDNES FLAT CROSSING, 1951. Engine No. 46423 is passing along the line from Warrington and is just crossing the original 1832 line to the docks. As can be seen from the point work, trains could pass from the east to the docks as well as from the west to the north, the latter being built in 1856. Controlling events is Widnes No. 4 box, just visible on the left. The usual vantage position for photographers was the long footbridge that connected Alforde Street to the canal.

CANAL CROSSING, WIDNES, 1965. Taking the original line across the swing bridge is Black Five 4-6-0 No. 44792. In front of it were extensive sidings by the docks, from which these wagons were loaded into barges. When these docks opened a price war developed. The canal shipped 45 tons for the price of 40, while the railway dropped their price by 10 per cent: the colliery owners were the gainers. The disadvantage suffered by the railways was that the load had to be transferred to their wagons and then onto barges at the docks. In fact, so precarious was their position, that in the first part of 1839 the line made a £500 loss.

FLAT CROSSING, 1961. Stanier 8F 2-8-0 No. 48729 negotiates the crossing on its way past No. 4 box. In front of it is the curve down from the deviation and the connection to the engine shed, which is probably its destination. It is seen here traversing the line from St Helens which had numerous connections to local industries. The Ditton-Warrington crossing illustrates the operational problems for a system of any complexity.

When Stanier took over CME for the LMSR in 1932 there was a yawning gap in the company's fleet for a good versatile heavy frieght loco, although they had produced the Beyer-Garette that hauled the very heavy coal trains onto the Midland division to London. They had also built 175 0-8-0s to replace the aging LNWR G class engines. However, both classes had serious maintenance problems, the faulty Midland Railway axle box was perpetuated. Also, goods services were undergoing a gradual acceleration necessitating a new loco.

Eventually the 852s were built, many by outside contractors, and they became widespread throughout the rail system. During the war many went to Europe and some to the Middle East. This example was built at Brighton in September 1944, and was painted unlined black.

ANNE STREET, 1960. Viewed south from the level crossing is the 1832 line to Runcorn Gap. Under the bridge, three more bridges can be made out and in the distance is the footbridge with its mid air junctions. The wagons are under the loop line to Tanhouse Lane and Central Stations. The ex-LNWR deviation line is the nearest bridge. On the left can be made out a 20 mph speed restriction sign which refers to the curve up to meet the deviation. Behind this is the point work to access the engine shed. Twelve years after being built at Crewe, caprotti valve geared Black Five 4-6-0 No. 44741 waits at the level crossing. This Ivatt modification of the Stanier design did little for its appearence. However, the experiences of the valve gear enabled it to be incorporated into some Standard Class engines, namely, 73125-54 and the celebrated *Duke of Gloucester*, No. 71000. The experimentation with the Black Five class extended to things other than the valve gear. While the example had standard plain bearing axle boxes, others had Timken roller bearing axle boxes, or SKF parallel-roller bearings, some on single axles, some on all axles, including the tender.

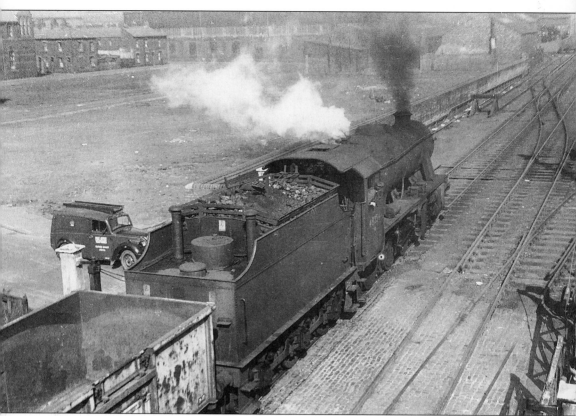

ANNE STREET, 1960. This was taken from the footbridge across the line, looking north. The scenery is typical of the line and illustrates the reason for its existence: industry. To the right was the gas works, still fed with coal as North Sea Gas was only just being piped into a national distribution network. Prior to that each town supplied its own gas from mostly isolated industries with no need to be connected. On the left are the premises of Widnes Foundry, the cleared land once had an aptly named row of houses there called Railway Street. The level crossing joined together the east and west parts of Anne Street. Passing north to St Helens with a train of empty coal wagons is 8F No. 48254. After being built by the North British Loco Co. in 1940, it saw war service overseas; the tender at this time was one from a green Jubilee Class engine. Here, and at several other places along the line, the LNWR opened a Rail Motor Halt from 1 October 1911, in an attempt to get more passengers. This scene is part of Ashley Way – the A562.

ANNE STREET CROSSING, WIDNES NO. 2 BOX, 1973. The gates across the street were replaced in the late 1960s by flashing lights and an 'open' crossing and the footbridge was replaced by a concrete and brick construction. Around the turn of the century the footbridge was on the other side of Anne Street and the box was on the other side of the line. The type of jobs that this thirty-five lever box controlled included the junction to the docks and up to the deviation, as well as local industries such as boiler works and Widnes Foundry.

NORTH OF ANNE STREET, 1980. The scene is almost thirty years after passenger services ceased and yet there is still a healthy business in coal traffic going south. By this time the line was single and at the Widnes end it became double at Tanhouse Lane Junction. Class 40 diesel loco No. 40.044 is clearing the single line from Sutton Oak Junction, while sister engine No. 40.026 waits to go north. In steam days freight trains often needed help up this 1 in 70 gradient; these locos had no such need of the Vine Banker.

WIDNES NO. 1 SIGNAL BOX, 1976. This box, one of eight in the area, was just south of the Warrington Road Bridge, visible in the background. Its twenty-five levers controlled the lines to the industries in the north of Widnes, including the gas works, Widnes Alkali Works and Tharsis Sulphur and Copper works, to name just a few. Of typical LNWR brick base and timber cabin design, it lasted until 1982.

TANHOUSE LANE SPUR, 1977. In 1961 a single track chord was opened from the St Helens' line to Tanhouse Lane on the GC and MR loop. This allowed the transfer of engines between the two systems, but the major reason was to enable chemical trains from Long Meg, on the Settle-Carlisle line, to get to the USAC factory near Tanhouse Lane. The Cement Manufacturing Company depot at Tanhouse Lane had trains from Leek, augmented by 1,000 ton trains from Kent. In 1982 a connection from Tanhouse Lane to the deviation near to Carterhouse Junction, enabled this chord and the remains of the St Helens' line to be closed.

APPLETON, 1963. The original St Helens' line had a severe operating problem from the day it opened. Not only was the line single (doubled throughout in 1850) but there were two inclined planes that had to be overcome. One was over the Liverpool-Manchester line at Sutton and the other was here, north of Widnes. They were both operated by stationary steam engines and imposed a restriction of six to seven loaded wagons at a time, so restricting traffic. In 1847 the Sutton incline was reduced to a gradient of 1 in 94/105. However, as illustrates the perilous state of the railway's finances, the company expected to make a loss in 1848 and so the work was not undertaken until 1850. Having no trouble coming down the gradient on 12 October is Class 5 4-6-0 No. 44823 with a parcels from north of St Helens. Appleton Station is in the background.

APPLETON, 1963. Austerity 8F 2-8-0 No. 90724 trundles a freight south of Appleton Station on its way to Widnes. As a means of by-passing the busy Edge Hill area, trains from Garston docks came through here on their way north. This loco started life as War Dept. No. 79302, receiving its BR number in July 1950. After spells at Sowerby Bridge and Wakefield it settled at Aintree, where it was withdrawn some eighteen months later.

APPLETON STATION, 1961. Ten years after the passengers had gone, the platforms and station buildings are still intact. The signal posts had to be tall to aid sighting over Halton View Road. Although primarily a goods line, stations like this were open before 1850. Ten years earlier just over 26,000 passengers used the St Helens' lines. By 1850 this figure was approaching 200,000. The elimination of the two inclines and a consequential reduction in journey time from about 100 minutes to approximately 25 minutes, which incidentally, it remained until closure a century later, helped this substantial increase, as did the industrialisation of Widnes.

APPLETON STATION, 1962. Jubilee Class 4-6-0 No. 45581 *Bihar and Orissa* climbs the bank on the return journey to St Helens or Wigan with a train load of coal empties, probably from Garston.

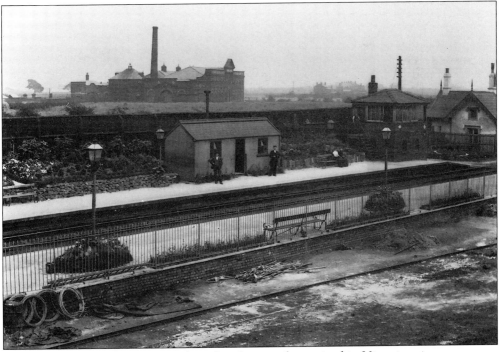

APPLETON STATION, 1895. When the photographer arrived in Victorian times, everyone turned out to pose for the shot. These well-kept platforms, complete with flower beds, illustrate the important standing of stations at the time.

FARNWORTH STATION, 1961. This site is very similar to Appleton, with its sparse housing surrounded by heavy industry, served by sidings from the main line. There was a 'small cottage and platform' at Bold, but it had a short life from being sanctioned in 1853, to closure in 1858. This station's name was changed on 2 January 1890, by the addition of '& Bold'. This view south, from the adjacent Derby Road Bridge, just fails to show the bridge this line makes over the CLC main line which, once a short tunnel, is now in a deep cutting.

FARNWORTH & BOLD, 1962. Going up the line to St Helens is Standard Class 2-6-0 No. 78017 on 1 January, leaking steam from everywhere. The coal yard appears to be in good use, only closing on 1 June 1964. The forty lever frame signal box is mounted on the platform. This station, along with Appleton and Sutton, had all opened by 1849. Additional station facilities in the form of 'a small cottage and platform' were authorised on 17 October 1853 but never appeared after *Bradshaw* of January 1858.

FARNWORTH & BOLD. Going north is a Cauliflower 0-6-0 in LNWR days. Apart from the alterations to the signal box the station remained basically unaltered until closure.

FARNWORTH & BOLD, 1961. Class Five No. 45446 going south approaches the now closed station. This was a daily parcels train from Carlisle to Wavertree (Liverpool). It used this line to go via Ditton Junction and so avoid a reversal at its journey's end.

UNION BANK FARM HALT. This, along with Anne Street, was opened on 1 October 1911 in an attempt to increase traffic, as also was the introduction of rail motors. These were no improvement on the auto trains such as the one shown here, which were later reverted to. The open construction of the platforms is interesting, complete with lamps.

CLOCK FACE, 1962. Looking south towards Widnes on 2 March sees Standard Class 2-6-0 No. 78035 passing by the colliery connections. To the left, now removed, were the lines to Clock Face Colliery. The signals are to allow the connection from Sutton Manor Colliery to go south.

CLOCK FACE COLLIERY SIGNAL BOX. Between Farnworth & Bold and Sutton Oak there were five such boxes in a little under a two-mile stretch of line. Not only were there sidings to collieries and the LNWR stores by the junction station, but there were also extensive sidings in both up and down directions. Much of the line was quadruple; alas, very little seems to have been recorded.

CLOCK FACE, 1962. This view looking north shows another part of the triangular connections that Sutton Manor Colliery had with the main Widnes to St Helens' line. Stanier 8F 2-8-0 No. 48249 is passing south with a load of coal hoppers. Its journey from Old Fold Colliery, east of St Helens, to Canada Dock, involved a journey across the main Liverpool to Manchester line to Widnes. There it would go via Speke Junction and Edge Hill to gain the LNWR's Bootle Branch to the docks.

CLOCK FACE STATION, 1957. Having just passed under Clock Face Lane the train is passing the rudimentary facilities on the Widnes platform. Opening in 1854, it was reduced to halt status from 12 July 1926, finally closing in 1951. While stations like these are regarded nostalgically by some people, it needs to be remembered that carrying passengers was definitely second fiddle to freight movement in the opinion of the railway companies in those early days. Indeed, in its infancy, it was custom and practise for passenger vehicles to be coupled at the end of a goods train. While official returns for 1838 show that over 26,000 passengers were carried, with five trains per day, it is reasonable to assume that each train carried less than ten passengers. As a result of the two inclines on the line, stationary engines hauled a small number of wagons up the 1 in 30 gradient at a time. It was remarked that a reasonably fit and healthy person who set off from St Helens when the train did, could get to Widnes in exactly the same time: 3 hours in 1835, 100 minutes in 1840 and 25 minutes once the incline planes had been eliminated.

CLOCK FACE, *c.* 1900. The platforms were staggered on either side of the road bridge; the St Helens' side had the 'small cottage and platform' described in the 1853 sanctioning. Part of the negotiations with the LNWR in 1851 made way for a south to east connection where the St Helens line crossed the L&M main line, but in the end this was never built. Sidings to allow exchanges between the companies were also discussed. The St Helens' Railway did buy fourteen acres of land which were used as the loco works, later they became a general store and sheeting works for the LNWR. Rails were also laid to Turner's glass works; both were accessible from the L&M line.

CLOCK FACE, 1964. South of the station, connections were built to collieries at Lea Green, Sutton Manor and Clock Face. A brick and timber LNWR twenty-five lever box controlled events. Standard class 9F 2-10-0 No. 92019 is seen passing north with empty limestone hoppers. They will have delivered their contents to the United Sulphuric Acid Company factory at Widnes and will be refilled at Long Meg sidings, Lazonby, on the Settle-Carlisle line. North of the station, extensive exchange sidings on both sides of the line were developed and the line quadrupled up to Sutton Oak Junction.

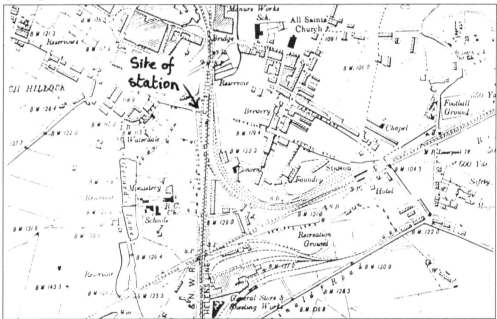

ROBINS LANE HALT. The original plan was for there to be four connections between the St Helens Railway and the Liverpool and Manchester main line. Due to economies only one, the north to east was built, and was the first section of the line open from 2 January 1832. The station on the main line was known as Sutton, but later officially became St Helens' Junction. In 1881 the simple curve joining the lines was altered. Two extra lines left the L&M, burrowed under the St Helens' line, and came up to join it at Sutton Oak Junction. It was on this joining line that Robins Lane Halt was opened on 12 October 1936. It was not a success and closed on 26 September 1938.

BROAD OAK, 1963. Bold power station forms the backdrop to this passenger service in the early 1960s. This view south from Sutton Road shows Dutch Barn Bridge from the other side with the St Helens' line passing straight on. The signal box is Broad Oak Junction and Sutton Oak engine shed was built in the fork. After the 1951 closure to passengers of the Widnes service, the main trains over the St Helens line were the push-pull service to Warrington, Bank Quay via Earlestown (See 1951 timetable extract on page 86). On 8 June, Stanier 2-6-2T No. 41286 is pushing its coaches towards St Helens with the 3.25 from Earlestown.

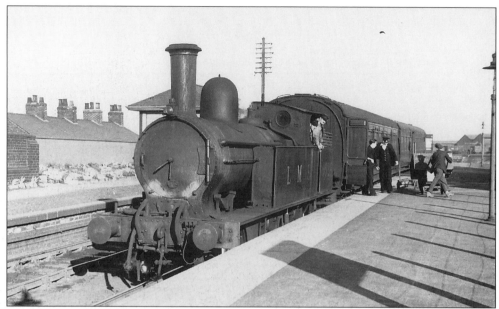

SUTTON OAK STATION, 1951. It is 6.25 on 26 April and Webb 2-4-2T No. (LMS) 6628 with push-pull coaches Nos 3441/3418 is on its way from Widnes with the 6.11 to St Helens. There, connections could be made to Wigan. Engines such as these or 0-6-2T plied the line from Ditton ('Junction' as it had became known since the early 1870s) to St Helens with, sometimes, four coach trains. The last train on the line was on 16 June 1951, when the 5.56 left St Helens, behind just such an engine.

SUTTON OAK STATION, c. 1950. Opening as 'Sutton', the suffix was added on 1 November 1864. The station consisted of a brick building on the St Helens' side and, later, the LNWR built the wooden facilities on the Widnes platform as this view north towards Dutch Barn Bridge shows. While morning and evening trains were busy, there was an eight hour period in the day with no trains. On Saturdays this gap was filled by a couple of trains at the expense of the morning and evening service.

SUTTON OAK SIGNAL BOX, 1979. This was the meeting place of the quadruple lines, both from St Helens' Junction in the east, and from Clock Face in the south. The line split, going west to St Helens and north. The latter direction in the early days of the operation was the meeting place for lines from several collieries in the area, namely, Ashtons Green, Broad Oak and Parr Stocks. Soon this was extended north across the St Helens' Canal to pits in the Blackbrook and Haydock areas. The single line was doubled in 1862 and later became part of the line to Carr Mill (avoiding St Helens) which opened on 23 February 1880. This closed as a through route in 1964 while, as pits were worked out, their lines were lifted. Controlling events there was this fine sixty-five lever all timber signal box. The absence of a standard LNWR brick base was company policy for buildings on ground liable to move – here due to mining subsidence. Adjacent was the Sutton Manure Works!

BROAD OAK JUNCTION SIGNAL BOX. This forty-four lever box controlled not only the entrance to Sutton Oak loco shed, but also the single line east to Peasley New Junctions. From there lines went south to Sutton Oak Junction and north to Marsh's Sidings, joining the line north from Sutton Oak Junction. These triangles allowed engines from the many pits access to the loco shed without having to occupy the main lines.

SUTTON, 1962. Engineering works necessitate diversions. While the main line wasn't available, this train of vans has been north at Sutton Oak Junction and then west along the Peasley line. Standard Class 2-6-0 No. 76077 is rounding the bend north of the engine shed to rejoin the main line at Broad Oak Junction.

SUTTON OAK LOCO SHED. An engine shed was built here in 1880 to replace the St Helens' Railway's shed just south of the L&M line at Clock Face, and a small shed at St Helens' Junction. Originally it was known as Peasley Cross; quite when it had a name change is uncertain. The ten road shed had a typical LNWR northlight roof which was replaced by a louvre style in 1946. This view looking south-east shows the water and, still manual coaling facilities, with the turntable beyond them. The signals are for Sutton Oak Junction.

SHUNTING ENGINES, 1951. At this time, three such 0-4-0 Sentinel shunting engines called Sutton Oak shed 10E, 'home'. The war time practise of painting objects white to prevent accidents is still evident. Interestingly, while both have their BR numbers, the larger engine has also got the new company logo. In contrast, Webb Tank, hauling passenger trains on the same day, still had its LMS number. Engine No. 47180 was built in 1930 and had a two-speed gear box.

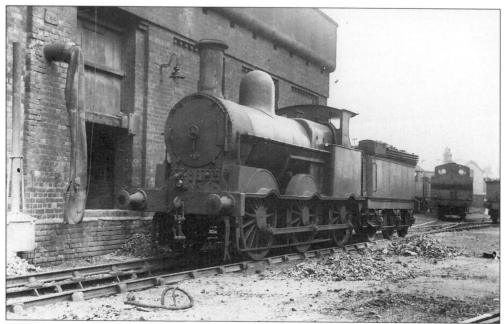

SUTTON OAK'S ENGINE SHED ALLOCATION. Cauliflower engines were very common up to the Second World War, both for short trip and shunting. Number 8549 waits adjacent to the water tank with the 1939 method of obtaining fuel from the 'coal hole' on show.

TURNTABLE, ST HELENS, 1957. In later days Ivatt tanks replaced the LNWR engines. No. 41286 is on the 60 ft turntable installed after the war to replace the ageing 42 ft one.

FREIGHT LOCOS, 1938. These ranged from short trips, as hauled by 0-6-0s, to long distance engines, like G Class No. 9303. Later, Moguls, firstly the LMS Black Pigs variety, then Standard Class engines took over many duties. Oddly enough Stanier 8Fs seem to have been rare here.

PASSENGER LOCOS. Passenger trains were handled by small tanks such as Webbs 2-4-2s, or by Coal Tanks, like No. 7778. In this pre-war photograph the northlight roof appears in good repair.

PEASLEY CROSS, 1963. Looking north from Sutton Road Bridge on 8 June, Stanier 2-6-2T No. 41286 can be seen on its way south, close to the site of the former Peasley Cross Station. It has just passed under Manor Street footbridge and the German style, variable pressure, constant volume gasometer dominates the sky-line. Possible destinations were Warrington, St Helens' Junction, Earlestown or Newton-le-Willows. With cross Pennine trains stopping at the last two as well as London, and trains to the north stopping at Warrington, quite a variety of passenger movements were possible: today's planners would relish such potential.

ST HELENS' GAS WORKS WAGON. Heating coal, in the absence of air, produced our domestic supply for almost ninety years and black tanks like these were built to transfer the useful by products for the chemical industry. St Helens' gasworks was by the Warrington Road, north of Peasley Cross Junction. This was the site of the meeting of some of the original lines from Cowley Hill, Rushy Park and Gerard's Bridge pits in the north, and the Ravenhead branch to the west. With the development of St Helens' third passenger station north of Raven Street and a link from here, single at first but doubled in 1856, to Gerard's Bridge, an alternative route existed to the east of the St Helens' Station.

74

PRIVATE OWNER'S WAGONS. Specialist wagons were built to carry not only raw materials such as sand to make glass, but also to transport away the finished product, in this case, plate glass.

The outbreak of war in 1939 spelled the beginning of the end of the P.O. wagon; utility reared its ugly head and the original glories were painted over. With the formation of the National Coal Board in 1948, the vast majority of such wagons became obsolete. Apart from advertising, there was a commercial reason for having private wagons. The railwy companies charged reservation charges for their wagons. Owners' wagons could be held at factories, sidings etc., far as long as was necessary without such charges.

RAVENHEAD JUNCTION, 1983. This was the meeting place of two of the original branches, west to Ravenhead Colliery and north to Gerard's Bridge. The expansion of industries such as St Helens' Crown Glass Works (from 1827), metal extractors and numerous alkali works, meant that along with the growth in coal mining, there was a vast proliferation of sidings and railway connections, many culminating in the Ravenhead and Eccleston branches joining the main line at Ravenhead Junction. Looking south along the branch, the main line passes from left to right. Semaphore signals, controlled by this twenty lever box, are still very much in evidence.

MARSH'S CROSSING, 1971. Typical of the numerous road crossings in the area is this small LNWR signal cabin with its fifteen levers. The gates would have been operated by hand. In the background is the line from St Helens to Huyton and Liverpool.

ST HELENS' PASSENGER STATIONS. On 25 September 1965 the LCGB organised a brake van tour of the St Helens area. The conflict seen here between trains, road vehicles and pedestrians has changed little from the days of the original station. This was a terminus, south-east of the canal, close to where the Warrington Old Road is now. Up to 1835 a horse-drawn carriage went between St Helens and the junction with the Liverpool and Manchester line. Later, passenger coaches were attached to the rear of freight trains whenever possible. The heavy freight traffic along the Ravenhead branch, and the number of level crossings, encouraged the directors to look for a new site. St Helens' first railway station, described as a 'small, rudely constructed wooded erection', stood on the southerly side of the ill-fated Kurtz Chemical works which blew up in May 1899 with the loss of eight lives and many injured.

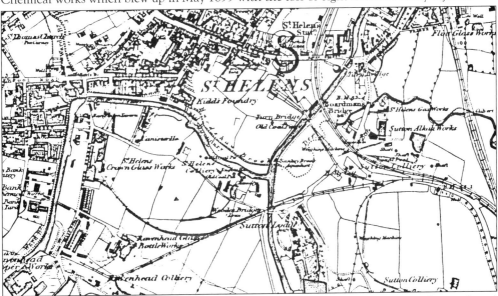

ST HELENS' THIRD STATION. To cope with trains approaching both from the north and the south, a connection was made to Gerard's Bridge and so the Rainford line. The opening of the line from Wigan, on 1 December 1869, joined the Rainford branch at Gerard's Bridge Junction and so services could be assimilated easily into this station. Local opinion was that the station was, 'a wretched little hole' and no one was sad to see it swept away by a larger one on the same site a few years later.

ST HELENS' SECOND STATION. From 1849 the canal was crossed and a new terminus station opened south of Raven Street on 19 December. This view across the canal towards the signal box shows the site of the second station.

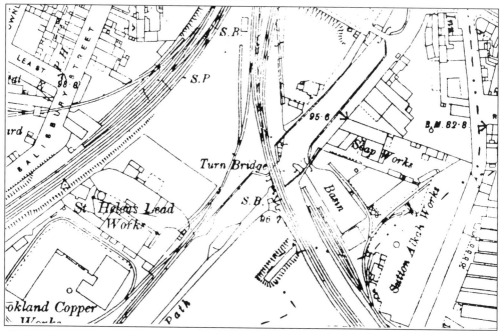

1891 MAP EXTRACT. This shows the bridge from which the adjacent view was taken. The signal box shows up well, as does the basin in which the barges were moored.

KURTZ CHEMICAL WORKS, 1900. This view is south, across the railway line and canal to the works with a number of barges in the basin. To the right is the 1849 canal crossing to the site, in the foreground, of the terminus station which opened on 19 December. With the development of the Rainford branch in the north, an operational problem existed. Trains from this branch would have to reverse in and out of the station. A new through station was therefore built north of the bridge, to be called Raven Street (now Parr Street); it opened on 1 February 1858. The old (1849) station became a coal yard. The signal box was replaced in 1902 by No. 3, which was at right angles, for better vision.

ST HELENS' FOURTH STATION, SHAW STREET, *c.* 1950. On 1 January 1872, a line from Huyton Junction and Liverpool opened from the east to the new station. It was re-named Shaw Street from 1 March 1949, as BR now had two stations in the same town – even if the other one was called Central. This view is south and it shows the line to Huyton off to the right and to Widnes to the left. The signal box visible under the bridge is No. 3, with its fifty-four levers. In its hey-day there were two platform faces and two bays. This view is along the two through lines and the size of the roof gives an indication of how important the station was to the railways, it actually made the site quite dark and gloomy. Note the water column on the down platform. The BR upper quadrant signals have not long replaced LNWR lower ones.

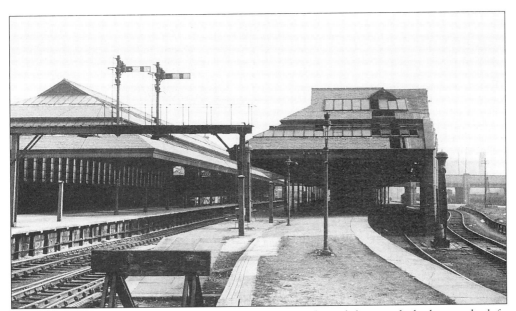

SHAW STREET, 1951. This view looks north along the through lines with the bay on the left. The roof seems to be in good condition; by the end of the decade it had been removed. The booking office was by the entrance, on the left. Note the water column on the right.

SHAW STREET, 1951. This aging 2-4-2T loco of the 910 Class introduced by the LNWR in the late 1890s is waiting to go to Warrington. The brick wall of the bay platform, together with the tiled roof, give an extremely gloomy appearance.

ST HELENS' SHAW STREET, 1961. Just arriving is a DMU on a service from Warrington. The glazed and tiled canopy which gave plenty of passenger protection was soon to come down. Around this time, train services in the area underwent one of their biggest shake ups. The arrival of such trains not only speeded up services, but was the start of some attempt at a regular pattern.

SHAW STREET, 1963. Stanier 2-6-2T No. 41286 has been given the clear road to set off with the 3.02 to Earlestown on 8 June. There was another terminus line to the right of the one occupied which had an engine release facility at the end. The bridge in the background, Corporation Street (formerly Sharp Street), was built so that these two lines could be extended under it northwards. The extreme right-hand bridge carries the St Helens' Canal. By now the track for the bay has been lifted. It would have been a waiting place for the shorter Widnes trains before their withdrawal in 1951.

ST HELENS' FIFTH STATION, 1965. In an attempt to get more passengers and better facilities, £80,000 was spent on refurbishment with stained glass a major feature. The platforms are very long and wide, considering the trains that used it. On the left, in platform one, is the DMU for Earlestown. It must be remembered that with the closure of collieries and the reduction in rail-borne traffic in the area, the previous avoiding lines were being taken up. Consequently, the through lines had to be kept clear and so the bays were needed. This view south illustrates the 'modern' approach: glass subway walls and see-through waiting areas.

ST HELENS' STATION, EXTERIOR, 1965. There is not a double yellow line in sight in this 1965 scene! The station is still in operation today, but has been known as 'Central' since 17 November 1971 to distinguish it from the 'Junction' – that isn't. Corporation Street is the bridge in the background, from which the previous photograph was taken.

ST HELENS,1961. This was taken from the road bridge, looking north in March, and it shows the extensive sidings full of wagons. Standard class 4 2-6-0 No. 76079 is organising wagons in the up goods loop. To the left is the large goods shed looking busy. The DMU has just come from Wigan and, after stopping at Shaw Street Station, will proceed to Liverpool, Lime Street. In the down goods loop is Patriot 4-6-0 No. 45516 *The Bedfordshire and Hertfordshire Regiment* with a train of non-corridor push-pull coaches that has just made the eighteen minute journey from Warrington. The rugby league supporters now face a twenty-five minute walk to Knowsley Road to see their team The Saints play. This was obviously in the days before mass car ownership!

ST HELENS' NO. 2 SIGNAL BOX, 1962. Between Sharp Street (now Corporation Street) and Pocket Nook Lane and Standish Street, was a series of sidings and a goods yard containing a large shed, two cranes and a cattle dock. Controlling events on these lines, as well as the lines north from the station, was this dilapidated, typical LNWR type 3 signal box. Refurbished, and now called Station, this is the only one still standing, although the original twenty-four levers have been reduced in number. Shunting in the yard is Class Five 4-6-0 No. 45270. Number 1 box was to the north, adjacent to the bridge in the background. Presumably, sighting pressures led to the multiple arms on the bracket.

Table 136 — 1951

ST. HELENS (SHAW STREET) AND WIDNES — Weekdays only.

Third Class Only (except where otherwise shown).

Miles.		SX	A		SO	SO	SX	SX	
		a. m.	a. m.	a. m.	p. m.	p. m.	p. m.	p. m.	p. m.
0	**St. Helens Shaw St.** ....dep.	6 20	6 47	8 25	12 42	1 15	4 37	5 20	5 56
¾	Peasley Cross	6 22	...	8 27	12 44	1 17	4 39	5 22	5 58
1¼	Sutton Oak	6 25	6 51	8 29	12 46	1 19	4 41	5 24	6 0
2¾	Clock Face	6 30	6 56	8 33	12 50	1 23	4 45	5 28	6 4
4¼	Union Bank Farm	6 34	.	8 37	12 54	1 27	4 49	5 32	6 8
5¼	Farnworth & Bold	6 38	7 3	8 40	12 57	1 30	4 52	5 36	6 12
6¼	Appleton	6 41	7 6	8 43	1 0	1 33	4 55	5 39	6 15
7	Ann Street	6 44	...	8 46	1 3	1 36	4 58	5 42	6 18
7¼	**Widnes** ....arr.	6 47	7 12	8 49	1 6	1 39	5 1	5 45	6 21
13	113 Warrington (Bank Quay)......arr.	...	7 48	...	...	...	5 29	...	7 6
9	113 **Ditton Junction** ....arr.	6 51	7 20	8 56	1 12	1 43	5 11	5 50	6 26
11½	96 Runcorn .... „	7 12	7 57	...	1 36	2 7	5 21	6 3	7 3
19¼	96 Liverpool (Lime Street) ...... „	7 40	8 15	9F37	1 59	2 23	5 59	6 26	7D36

Miles.		SX	A	SO	SO	SX	SX		SX
		a. m.	a. m.	a. m.	p. m.	p. m.	p. m.	p. m.	p. m.
—	96 Liverpool (Lime Street) ......dep.	5 55	7 10	10 45	1 5	3 27	.	5 5	5 32
—	96 Runcorn .... „	6 14	7 28	p. m.	1 15	...	...	5H19	5 49
—	113 **Ditton Junction** .... „	7 0	8 0	12 15	1 32	4 10	.	5 34	6 8
—	113 Warrington (Bank Quay)......dep.	...	7 48	...	12 16	...	...	5 15	...
0	**Widnes** ....dep.	7 3	8 7	12 18	1 37	4 16	5 8	5 37	6 11
¼	Ann Street	7 5	...	12 20	1 39	4 18	5 9	5 39	6 13
1	Appleton	7 8	8 11	12 23	1 42	4 21	5 12	5 42	6 16
2	Farnworth & Bold	7 11	8 15	12 26	1 45	4 24	5 15	5 45	6 19
3	Union Bank Farm	7 14	.	12 29	1 48	4 27	...	5 48	6 22
4½	Clock Face	7 18	8 22	12 33	1 52	4 31	5 22	5 52	6 26
6	Sutton Oak	7 22	8 26	12 37	1 56	4 36	5 26	5 56	6 31
6½	Peasley Cross	7 24	...	12 39	1 58	4 38	5 28	5 58	6 33
7¼	**St. Helens Shaw St.** ....arr.	7 28	8 31	12 43	2 2	4 42	5 36	6 2	6 37

A—Conveys First and Third Class passengers, Saturdays excepted.
D—On Saturdays arrives Liverpool (Lime Street) 7.12 p.m.
F—On Saturdays arrives Liverpool (Lime Street) 10.31 a.m.
H—On Saturdays departs Runcorn 5.14 p.m.
SO—Saturdays only.
SX—Saturdays excepted.

For other trains between St. Helens Shaw Street and Sutton Oak, see Table 128.

1951 TIMETABLE EXTRACT. In those post-war times, still subject to rationing and general austerity, it was not surprising that no one travelled on week days between 8.00 am and 4.00 pm. Today's much more affluent and mobile society would require at least hourly trains, with good connections.

Four

Ormskirk and Rainford to St Helens

The line from St Helens to Rainford was constructed in response to the 1851 plans proposed by the Southport and St Helens' Railway in order to encroach upon territory, rightfully regarded as their own, by the St Helens' Canal and Railway. While the latter had lines to Cowley Hill and other collieries to the north of St Helens from 1832, they had done nothing more. The response in 1852 was to suggest the just over 6 mile line to meet the L&Y at Rainford. The East Lancashire Railway also received the power to extend their Ormskirk to Skelmersdale line to Rainford, although it would be 1858 before both branches carried traffic. There was an earlier plan in the 'Railway Mania' days, for a triangle on the Southport to Euxton line, near Rufford, to pass near to Ormskirk, Skelmersdale and Rainford, ending at a terminus in St Helens. Like so many others, it never materialised.

L&Y AUTO COACH NO. 8. Services using these trains radiated out from Ormskirk to Southport, Town Green and Rainford. As the halts had very rudimentary facilities, a set of steps was attached to the middle door which were capable of being let down to let passengers get on. Note the L&Y name and crest appear on its sides. Aspinall 2-4-2T with auto fitted trains took over in around the 1930s.

ORMSKIRK STATION, c. 1900. The station, on the line from Walton Junction Liverpool, to Preston, was to be opened by the East Lancashire Railway, but by 2 April 1849 it had been absorbed by the L&Y. This view is from the Preston platform, looking towards Liverpool. That platform was longer because it had bays at both ends; a coach, probably an auto train, is in the down one. The fine footbridge and the different canopies show up well. Electrification reached here in 1913. The pattern of services that developed was for the electrics to be 'all stations', while the longer distance trains stopped here, so allowing interchange of passengers.

ORMSKIRK STATION, 1906. To cope with the expected levels of traffic the L&Y developed these rail motor trains. The presence of the photographer suggests that this was taken at the inauguration of the service in July 1906 and shows 0-4-0T No. 9. The station name board makes interesting reading. To the rear of the train can be made out the L&Y parachute water tank at the end of the Preston platform. Also on that platform is the not long (1900) opened eighty lever frame signal box.

ORMSKIRK ENGINE SHED AFTER CLOSURE. Along with extensive sidings, loco servicing facilities were developed between the branch and the main line. Although this four road engine shed was built in 1893, it wasn't the first, the 1876 shed was destroyed by fire, but this one lasted until 1935. The photographer was standing in the Preston lines with the Rainford branch on the other side of the water tank and coal hole. There was a 50 ft turntable between the two structures.

BAY PLATFORM, ORMSKIRK, 1952. This bay platform is at the Preston end of the down platform. There used to be a red telephone booth at the end of the station buildings, near the bay. The probable purpose of the early 1900 wooden structure was to allow the rail motor trains to be refuelled in between journeys without them having to go to the shed, especially after it closed. Coal was shovelled from wagons in the bay onto the platform, and then into the coal bunker of the engine. The auto-train has arrived from Rainford behind Stanier 2-6-2T No. 41284 on 5 January.

ORMSKIRK TO RAINFORD JUNCTION. The destination board on Motor Train No. 5's coach reads, 'Ormskirk Rainford Junction & St. Helens'.

ORMSKIRK, 1939. Passing over the junction of the Rainford branch with the main line is unidentified ex-L&Y 0-8-0. The building to the right was a goods shed and the engine is obscuring the now closed engine shed. It was at about this point that Aspinall 1400 Class 4-4-2 No. 702 collided with a Radial Tank No. 1470 on 25 November 1910. Consequently, 702s main frames, by the smoke box, were straight instead of curved.

Table 129

ST. HELENS (SHAW STREET), RAINFORD JUNCTION AND ORMSKIRK

THIRD CLASS ONLY

1951

WEEKDAYS

Miles		a.m.	a.m.	a.m.	a.m.	a.m.	a.m.	SO a.m.	SO a.m.	SO a.m.	p.m.	SO p.m.	SO p.m.	p.m.		SX p.m.	p.m.	p.m.	p.m.	p.m.	p.m.	SO p.m.	SO p.m.	SO p.m.	SX p.m.	SO p.m.
—	126 Liverpool (L.S.) (via Prescot) dep.	...	...	6 0	...	7 15	...	...	...	11 5	...	...	1 20	...	...	3 20	...	4 17	...	5 25	...	6 0	...	...	...	...
—	125 Warrington (Bank Quay) dep.	.	.	.	.	7 20	.	.	.	10 45	.	.	1 5	.	.	2 18	.	4 25	.	5 23	.	.	.	.	.	.
0	**St. Helens Shaw St.** dep.	6 27	...	7 0	...	8 0	...	...	...	p.m. 12 10	...	...	1 57	...	...	4 12	...	5 3	...	6 7	...	6 57	...	...	...	...
1¼	Moss Bank	6 30	.	7 3	.	8 3	.	.	.	12 13	.	.	2 0	.	.	4 15	.	5 6	.	6 10	.	7 0	.	.	.	.
2¼	Crank Halt	6 33	...	7 6	...	8 6	...	...	...	12 16	...	...	2 3	...	...	4 18	...	5 9	...	6 13	...	7 3	...	...	...	...
3	Old Mill Lane	6 35	.	7 8	.	8 8	.	.	.	12 18	.	.	2 5	.	.	4 20	.	5 11	.	6 15	.	7 5	.	.	.	.
3¼	Rookery	6 37	...	7 10	...	8 10	...	...	...	12 20	...	...	2 7	...	...	4 22	...	5 13	...	6 17	...	7 7	...	...	...	...
4¼	Rainford Village	6 40	.	7 13	.	8 13	.	.	.	12 23	.	.	2 10	.	.	4 25	.	5 16	.	6 20	.	7 10	.	.	.	.
5¼	**Rainford Junction** arr.	6 45	...	7 18	...	8 18	...	...	...	12 28	...	...	2 15	...	...	4 30	...	5 21	...	6 25	...	7 15	...	...	...	...
—	124 Wigan (Wallgate) arr.	.	.	7 40	.	8 44	.	.	.	12 49	.	.	2 38	.	.	4 53	.	5 44	.	6SX50	.	7 37	.	.	.	.
—	124 Liverpool (Exchange) arr.	7 40	...	8 12	...	9 11	...	...	...	1 1	...	...	...	...	...	5 0	...	6K13	...	...	...	7 59	...	...	...	...
—	124 Wigan (Wallgate) dep.	Stop	6 5	.	6 53	.	7 53	.	10 21	.	12 15	.	.	1 38	.	.	4 9	.	.	.	6 1	.	7 12	9 12	.	10 53
—	124 Liverpool (Exchange) dep.	...	5 50	...	6 55	...	7 55	...	9 18	...	11D40	12 42	...	1SO50	...	...	4 3	...	4 53	...	5 40	...	6 48	9 12	10 15	10 15
—	**Rainford** Junction dep.	.	6 55	.	7 40	.	8 25	.	10 55	.	12 40	1 30	.	2 20	.	.	4 39	.	5 30	.	6 30	.	7 35	9 43	10 50	11 20
6½	Hey's Crossing	...	6 58	...	7 43	...	8 28	...	10 58	...	12 43	1 33	...	2 23	...	...	4 42	...	5 33	...	6 33	...	7 38	9 46	10 53	11 23
7¼	White Moss Level Crossing	a.m.	7 1	.	7 46	.	8 31	.	11 1	.	12 46	1 36	.	2 26	.	.	4 45	.	5 36	.	6 36	.	7 41	9 49	10 56	11 26
8	Skelmersdale	6 5	7 3	...	7 48	...	8 33	9 30	11 3	...	12 48	1 38	...	2 28	...	...	4 47	...	5 38	...	6 38	...	7 43	9 51	10 58	11 28
9¾	Westhead	6 11	7 9	.	7 54	.	8 39	9 36	11 9	.	12 54	1 44	.	2 34	.	.	4 53	.	5 44	.	6 44	.	7 49	9 57	11 4	11 34
11¾	**Ormskirk** arr.	6 15	7 13	...	7 58	...	8 43	9 40	11 13	...	12 58	1 48	...	2 38	...	...	4 57	...	5 48	...	6 48	...	7 53	10 1	11 8	11 38
—	149 Preston arr.	6 58	.	.	8 43	.	9 41	10 36	12 4	.	2N17	2 30	.	3SO19	.	.	5 48	.	6 33	.	7 28	.	8 30	.	.	.
—	149 Southport (Chapel St.) ,,	...	8 5	...	9 6	...	10X 7	10 23	11 42	...	1H28	2 39	...	3 50	...	...	5 35	...	6 22	...	7SO27	...	8 22	10 59	...	a.m.
—	149 Liverpool (Exchange) ,,	6 58	7 43	.	8 32	.	9 23	10 13	11 53	.	1 33	2 21	.	3 8	.	.	5R33	.	6 23	.	7 23	.	8 28	10 38	.	12 13

SUNDAYS

Miles		p.m.	p.m.	p.m.	p.m.	p.m.	p.m.	p.m.	p.m.
—	126 Liverpool (L.S.) (via Prescot) dep.	...	...	...	...	...	...	...	...
—	125 Warrington (Bank Quay) dep.	.	.	.	.	.	.	.	.
0	**St. Helens Shaw St.** dep.	...	...	...	...	...	...	...	...
1¼	Moss Bank	.	.	.	.	.	.	.	.
2¼	Crank Halt	...	...	...	...	...	...	...	...
3	Old Mill Lane	.	.	.	.	.	.	.	.
3¼	Rookery	...	...	...	...	...	...	...	...
4¼	Rainford Village	.	.	.	.	.	.	.	.
5¼	**Rainford Junction** arr.	...	...	...	...	...	...	...	...
—	124 Wigan (Wallgate) arr.	.	.	.	.	.	.	.	.
—	124 Liverpool (Exchange) arr.	...	...	...	...	...	...	...	...
—	124 Wigan (Wallgate) dep.	.	.	.	5 36	.	.	9 42	10 35
—	124 Liverpool (Exchange) dep.	...	2 15	...	5 25	...	...	9 10	...
—	**Rainford** Junction dep.	1 25	2 50	5 5	6 10	7 40	9 25	10 15	11 0
6½	Hey's Crossing	1 28	2 53	5 8	6 13	7 43	9 28	10 18	11 3
7¼	White Moss Level Crossing	1 31	2 56	5 11	6 16	7 46	9 31	10 21	11 6
8	Skelmersdale	1 33	2 58	5 13	6 18	7 48	9 33	10 23	11 8
9¾	Westhead	1 39	3 4	5 19	6 24	7 54	9 39	10 29	11 14
11¾	**Ormskirk** arr.	1 43	3 8	5 23	6 28	7 58	9 43	10 33	11 18
—	149 Preston arr.	.	.	.	7 40	10 0	.	.	.
—	149 Southport (Chapel St.) ,,	2 19	...	...	7 10	...	10 17	...	...
—	149 Liverpool (Exchange) ,,	2 23	4 13	6 13	7 23	8 53	10 10	11 13	11 53

WEEKDAYS

Miles		a.m.	a.m.	a.m.	a.m.	a.m.	a.m.	a.m.	SO p.m.	SO p.m.	p.m.	SO p.m.		p.m.	SX p.m.	p.m.	p.m.	SO p.m.	SX p.m.	p.m.	SO p.m.	SO p.m.	SO p.m.		p.m.	SO p.m.	
—	149 Liverpool (Exchange) dep.	6 0	...	6 35	...	7 30	...	11 20	12 25	...	1 15	...	...	3 35	...	4 25	...	5 10	5 19	...	6 15	...	8 25	...	9 55	10 55	...
—	149 Southport (Chapel St.) ,,	.	.	6 37	.	7 21	.	.	12 10	.	1 13	.	.	.	.	4 15	.	5 5	5 5	.	6 5	.	8 40	.	9 50	10 40	.
—	149 Preston ,,	...	...	...	...	6 55	...	10SO20	12 15	...	1 10	...	...	2 40	...	3B40	...	5 12	5 12	...	5 43	...	7 18	...	9 20	10 55	...
0	**Ormskirk** dep.	6 26	.	7 20	.	8 5	.	12 0	1 5	.	1 55	.	.	4 10	.	5 6	.	5 50	6 0	.	6 57	.	9 21	.	10 30	11 45	.
1½	Westhead	6 30	...	7 24	...	8 9	...	12 4	1 9	...	1 59	...	...	4 14	...	5 10	...	5 54	6 4	...	7 1	...	9 25	...	10 34	11 49	...
3¼	Skelmersdale	6 36	.	7 30	.	8 15	.	12 10	1 15	.	2 5	.	.	4 20	.	5 16	.	6 0	6 10	.	7 7	.	9 31	.	10 40	11 55	.
4	White Moss Level Crossing	6 38	...	7 32	...	8 17	...	12 12	1 17	...	2 7	...	...	4 22	...	5 18	...	6 2	6 12	...	7 9	...	9 33	...	10 42	...	...
4¾	Hey's Crossing	6 41	.	7 35	.	8 20	.	12 15	1 20	.	2 10	.	.	4 25	.	5 21	.	6 5	6 15	.	7 12	.	9 36	.	10 45	.	.
6	**Rainford** Junction arr.	6 44	...	7 38	...	8 23	...	12 18	1 23	...	2 13	...	...	4 28	...	5 24	...	6 8	6 18	...	7 15	...	9 39	...	10 48	...	...
—	124 Liverpool (Exchange) arr.	7 40	.	8 12	.	9 11	.	1 1	2 24	.	.		.	5 0	.	6K13	.	6 47	6 47	.	7 59	.		.	11SO43	.	.
—	124 Wigan (Wallgate) arr.	7 40	...	...	...	8 44	...	1F28	...	...	2SO38	...	...	4 48	...	5 44	...	6 30	6 50	...	7 37	...	10 1	...	...	...	...
—	124 Liverpool (Exchange) dep.	A.	5 50	.	6 55	.	7 55	.	.	12 42	.	1 50	.	.	4 3	.	4 53	.	.	5 40	.	6 48	.	.	.	.	.
—	124 Wigan (Wallgate) ,,	...	6 5	...	7 21	...	7 53	...	...	12 15	...	1 38	...	...	4 9	...	...	...	...	6 1	...	7 10	...	...	...	...	...
—	**Rainford Junction** dep.	.	6 48	.	7 43	.	8 34	.	.	1 28	.	2 20	.	.	4 40	.	5 35	.	.	6 30	.	7 34	.	.	.	.	.
7	Rainford Village	...	6 50	...	7 45	...	8 36	...	...	1 30	...	2 22	...	...	4 42	...	5 38	...	...	6 33	...	7 37	...	...	...	...	...
7¾	Rookery	.	6 52	.	7 47	.	8 38	.	.	1 32	.	2 24	.	.	4 44	.	5 40	.	.	6 35	.	7 39	.	.	.	.	.
8½	Old Mill Lane	...	6 54	...	7 49	...	8 40	...	...	1 34	...	2 26	...	...	4 46	...	5 42	...	...	6 37	...	7 41	...	...	...	...	...
9	Crank Halt	.	6 59	.	7 52	.	8 43	.	.	1 37	.	2 29	.	.	4 49	.	5 45	.	.	6 40	.	7 44	.	.	.	.	.
9¾	Moss Bank	...	7 1	...	7 54	...	8 45	...	...	1 39	...	2 31	...	...	4 51	...	5 47	...	...	6 42	...	7 46	...	...	...	...	...
11¼	**St. Helens Shaw St.** arr.	.	7 6	.	7 59	.	8 50	.	.	1 44	.	2 36	.	.	4 56	.	5 51	.	.	6 46	.	7 50	.	.	.	.	.
—	125 Warrington (Bank Quay) arr.	...	...	...	8 46	...	9 27	...	...	3 25	...	5 48	...	...	5 54	...	7SX19	...	...	8 4	...	9 27	...	...	...	...	...
—	126 Liverpool (L.S.) (via Prescot) ,,	.	7 52	.	8 50	.	9A45	.	.	2 57	.	4 44	.	.	5 42	.	7 9	.	.	8A18	.	9 2	.	.	.	.	.

SUNDAYS

Miles		p.m.	p.m.	p.m.	p.m.	p.m.	p.m.	p.m.	p.m.
—	149 Liverpool (Exchange) dep.	12 32	1 15	3 40	4 45	6 45	8 10	9 15	10 40
—	149 Southport (Chapel St.) ,,	.	12 55	.	.	6 0	8 30	.	10 40
—	149 Preston ,,	...	1 45	3 30	4 13	5 40	8 15	9 7	10 2
0	**Ormskirk** dep.	1 5	2 25	4 20	5 30	7 10	9 2	9 52	11 25
1½	Westhead	1 9	2 29	4 24	5 34	7 14	9 6	9 56	11 29
3¼	Skelmersdale	1 15	2 35	4 30	5 40	7 20	9 12	10 2	11 35
4	White Moss Level Crossing	1 17	2 37	4 32	5 42	7 22	9 14	10 4	...
4¾	Hey's Crossing	1 20	2 40	4 35	5 45	7 25	9 17	10 7	.
6	**Rainford** Junction arr.	1 23	2 43	4 38	5 48	7 28	9 20	10 10	...
—	124 Liverpool (Exchange) arr.	.	3 41	.	6 25	.	10 22	11 22	.
—	124 Wigan (Wallgate) arr.	...	3 2	...	6 11	...	9 59	...	...
—	124 Liverpool (Exchange) dep.	.	.	.	.	.	.	.	.
—	124 Wigan (Wallgate) ,,	...	...	...	...	...	...	...	...
—	**Rainford Junction** dep.	.	.	.	.	.	.	.	.
7	Rainford Village	...	...	...	...	...	...	...	...
7¾	Rookery	.	.	.	.	.	.	.	.
8½	Old Mill Lane	...	...	...	...	...	...	...	...
9	Crank Halt	.	.	.	.	.	.	.	.
9¾	Moss Bank	...	...	...	...	...	...	...	...
11¼	**St. Helens Shaw St.** arr.	.	.	.	.	.	.	.	.
—	125 Warrington (Bank Quay) arr.	...	...	...	...	...	...	...	...
—	126 Liverpool (L.S.) (via Prescot) ,,	.	.	.	.	.	.	.	.

A—Via St. Helens Junction. (Table 128).
B—On Saturdays departs Preston 4.25 p.m.
D—a.m. and on Saturdays departs Liverpool (Ex.) 12.5 p.m.
F—On Saturdays arrives Wigan (Wallgate) 12.49 p.m.
H—On Wednesdays arrives Southport (Chapel Street) 1.36 p.m.
K—On Saturdays arrives Liverpool (Exchange) 6.23 p.m.
N—On Saturdays arrives Preston 2.3 p.m.
R—On Saturdays arrives Liverpool (Ex.) 5.26 p.m.
SO—Saturdays only.
SX—Saturdays excepted.
X—On Saturdays arrives Southport (Chapel St.) 10.23 a.m.

TRAIN SERVICE, *c.* 1910. There was little passenger traffic along the line and, apart from Skelmersdale, no stations up till Rainford Junction. This extract from *Bradshaw* for 1910 shows not only the 'halts' en route, but also how the almost hourly service was operated. Note the smart turn around times at both Rainford and Ormskirk for the 'Skem Dodger', as it was affectionately known. Youngsters who use to go to Skelmersdale in the 1920s and '30s for jazz music evenings called it the 'Skem Jazzer'.

BLAGUEGATE COLLIERY. The main purpose of the line was to feed the number of collieries. Skelmersdale had up and down loops as well as an extensive series of sidings controlled by its South signal box. At Ormskirk there was a series of branch sidings and although there was limited accommodation for wagons at Rainford Junction, it should be remembered that with the direct connection to St Helens, trains could pass directly to the industries there, in Widnes, or to the docks.

SKELMERSDALE STATION, 1905. This was built adjacent to the main road, later the A577. The level crossing at the Ormskirk end had the controlling signal box and footbridge next to it. Although there were buildings on both platforms, only the Rainford platform had a canopy. Opening as Blaguegate, it changed its name in 1874 and while the halts closed in 1951, Skelmersdale staggered on until 5 November 1956, for passengers, not closing completely until 1963.

BUSHY LANE JUNCTION. Between Skelmersdale and Rainford Junction was White Moss Halt to serve the pit of the same name. Some time later, Heys Halt was established nearer to Rainford Junction. To enable coal trains to pass directly south, a single line was taken from the line into Rainford Junction. It passed over the main Liverpool to Wigan line and was joined, at Randle Junction, by the branch from Rainford Junction to St Helens. The original St Helens' Railway plan was for their line to pass under the L&Y to make an end on junction with the East Lancashire from Ormskirk. While most readers will be familiar with the white circle with a red stripe as shunting discs, few will know that some companies, such as the LNWR, used miniature signal arms for the same purpose. This view looking south shows the line to Rainford departing to the left and, carrying straight on, the single line to Randle Junction.

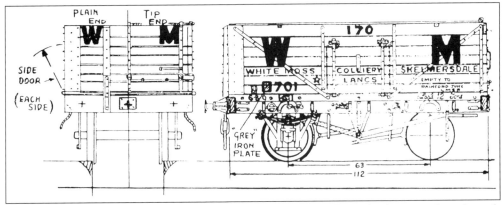

WHITE MOSS COLLIERY WAGON, 1924. The livery of this vehicle was red oxide with white letters which were sometimes embellished with black shading. The ironwork was black.

RAINFORD JUNCTION. This view from the signal box looks through the station to the east. The platforms look way out of proportion to the length of any trains that were scheduled to stop there, but their length allowed both main and branch trains to be on the same platform without obstructing each other. The main line trains stopped under the foot and road bridges. The fine junction signals have been hoisted well up to enable them to be seen clearly.

The contrasting railway companies' treatment of passengers is well illustrated by their opposing facilities. The L&Y side, on the left, has a fine set of stone buildings. The LNWR has a couple of wooden huts with a canopy between them! There was a signal on each long platform; this enabled passengers to change trains. The St Helens bound signal was replaced in later LMS days by an upper quadrant arm on a steel post.

RAINFORD. Although planned and developed by the Liverpool and Bury Railway, Rainford was opened by the L&Y on 20 November. It closed almost ten years later only to re-open a quarter of a mile east to accommodate branches from Ormskirk in the north, and St Helens in the south. It then became 'Junction', which survived until 1973 when it reverted to its original name. This view south along the main line from the footbridge shows an almost symmetrical site. The curving platforms serve St Helens, to the left, and Ormskirk, to the right. By the time of this photograph in 1965, both branches had lost their passenger services; the track to their respective bays has been lifted. In the background is the Bushy Lane to Randle Junction's line that allowed direct running from Ormskirk to St Helens.

RAINFORD JUNCTION, 1956. Just leaving the main line platform, bound for Liverpool, is Stanier 2-6-4T No. 42642, probably with the 11.59 am (SO) from Wigan to Liverpool. If this was the 3.45 from Bolton to Liverpool Exchange, arriving at 5pm, then there were plenty of opportunities for interchange at Rainford. Passengers to and from both Ormskirk and St Helens could have reached their destinations. With such stopping trains approximately every two hours, this type of service should have been standard. Alas, it was a rarity and so passengers preferred buses and cars. This, together with the decline in mining, led to the run down in services. The L&Y's expresses between the two counties use to storm through here until the early 1970s. As a nice touch, something, as well as 'LMR' is written in whitewashed stone.

SIGNALLING AT RAINFORD JUNCTION, 1987. While the brick base here is the original L&Y structure with the top re-built by the LMS in 1933, only ten of its eventual fifty-six levers are in use. The line towards Liverpool was singled to Fazackerley in 1970 and to Kirkby, to coincide with electrification, seven years later. Two car DMUs ply the route with a token being exchanged at the box.

LNWR SIGNALS. This post was situated at the end of the St Helens' platform. The top arm (St Helens' branch outer home) would have been pulled off by lever No. 44, while the lower arm was the distant signal for Randle Junction, just over a quarter of a mile to the south. The line was used up and down on the right hand track, with the left hand one used as a passing loop. The tiny bracket arm was for trains going straight on, up the freight only loop.

L&Y SIGNALS. Coming off the up Ormskirk branch were three sidings for the exchange of wagons between it and the main line. This concrete slotted post controlled the exit from them. The warning post illustrates that wagons, without their brakes pinned down, needed to be prevented from entering the running lines. In the days before track circuiting, unless the signalman could see the line, 'all clear' was not always true, and accidents could happen.

RAINFORD JUNCTION, 1952. Main line trains tended to stop briefly at the main platform, but the branch trains waited longer. To stop blocking the up line, Ormskirk trains tended to wait in the bay, as shown. There was much less traffic in the Wigan to St Helens direction so this pattern of service could be practised.

SIGNAL BOX INTERIOR, 1956. Probably very little had changed since this box opened in 1874. Above the shelf was the diagram of the lines controlled with the numbers and positions of the points and signals on it. The shelf has the block instruments which permitted coded communication to the next boxes along the lines. Dials indicated the state of line: free or occupied. The lever frame, set in the floor, has a wooden foot board to assist when pulling the numbered levers. Some of the rods and wires would need considerable effort to activate them. The windows face onto the main line.

RANDLE JUNCTION, 1956. This was the meeting place of two single lines. Straight on was the junction avoiding line from Bushey Lane; from the right, coming up the gradient, is the line from Rainford Junction. Controlling events was this small, twenty lever, rather run down LNWR signal box with a timber cabin on top of a brick base.

RAINFORD VILLAGE, 1962. The St Helens' Railway built the branch from Gerards Bridge in 1857. It wasn't until the start of the next year that they made plans for intermediate stations along the line; services started on 1 February. This station was originally called Rainford, the same name that the Liverpool & Bury had called their station which had opened some ten years earlier. To avoid confusion, this one was renamed Village in November 1861. The level crossing was south of the station.

RAINFORD VILLAGE, 1961. The tall, platform mounted box with twenty-seven levers not only controlled the level crossing, but also the merging of the two lines just north of the station. Its position would be to allow opening of the gates, while its height was to enable the joining of the two single lines to be seen. The St Helens' platform, on the left, had a wooden waiting room and shelter with a curved roof, similar to those further along the line, all built by a local builder.

ROOKERY. While the buildings carry the trade-mark of the line's builder, the wooden platforms reveal the station to be an afterthought, not opening for some months after the line was operational. This site was the second, located almost three quarters of a mile north of the original hut which was erected to see if there was any passenger traffic. There wasn't, so the halt closed in March 1862. This station opened on 1 June 1865.

CRANK. Having come to the end of its useful life, this was another late arrival on the line, opening at the end of 1858. The differing platform constructions are interesting. It had been an unstaffed halt since 1940. The road is the B5201, with the nearer signal post being ex-LNWR while the other is LMS.

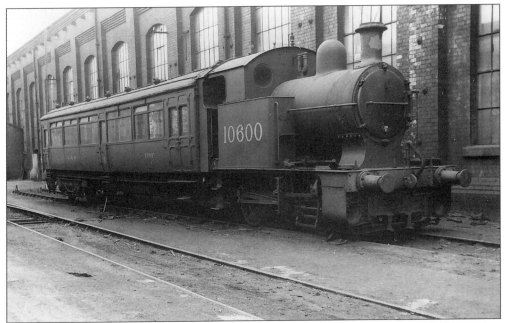

MOTOR TRAIN IN LMS DAYS. Although this unit is at Horwich, it was typical of those that plied the line from 1911 before being taken over by auto trains hauled by Aspinall 2-4-2T. Starting life in May 1906 as No. 3, this unit lasted until June 1947. When newly built, each coach bore the same number as the engine. However, maintenance of the coaches was carried out at Newton Heath, and the engines at Horwich. This resulted in units being out of action due to the coach of one, and the engine of another, being repaired. Subsequently, it was rare to see both parts having the same number.

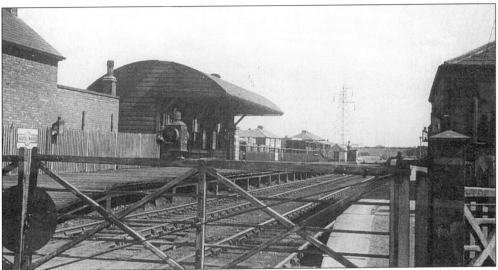

MOSS BANK STATION, 1950. The wooden shelter on the St Helens' platform makes this unmistakably one of the clones for the stations along the line. Moss Bank opened with the line in early 1858. The cattle trade was important here, hence the sidings on the down side. Like all the other passenger stations along the line, Moss Bank closed, in this case on 16 June 1951. A small, ten lever, platform mounted, ground frame by the crossing, controlled events until 1967.

MOSS BANK STATION, 1962. This view looking north to the level crossing shows the Rainford platform, where the main station facilities were. Since closure, the line was busy with excursions, summer trains and freight. On Valentine's Day, Stanier 8F 2-8-0 No. 48500 is passing with a Horbury to Garston freight train. The line here went down a 1 in 270 gradient to Gerard's Bridge Junction.

PILKINGTON'S SIDINGS. There was a sand washing facility here and this became the end of the line from St Helens in 1964. The business amounted to around 4,000-5,000 tons per week, necessitating Sunday workings. This too succumbed to road haulage and the line cut back to Cowley Hill in 1967, a position not far short of the original 1832 line! Shunting at the sidings is Stanier 8F 2-8-0 No. 48045. The twenty-lever box has the standard LNWR brick base and wooden top. A quarter of a mile south, where the line crossed the Rainford Brook, close to where one of the canal branches ended, was the site for Gerard's Bridge Station – one of the original stations dating from the opening of the line in 1858 and lasting until 1 August 1904.

Five
Huyton to St Helens

This line was built by the LNWR between 1868 and 1871; the outcrop of sandstone at Thatto Heath slowed down the work on this less than five mile line. The development of another station at St Helens, to replace that of 1858 – 'a standing disgrace to the town' – wasn't much better being called 'fourth class'. Rebuilt, it still survives today.

HUYTON STATION AND JUNCTION. This was one of the original stations on the Liverpool-Manchester line. As it was where the turnpike road to Warrington crossed the line, there was a protective gate. Thus the station was known as 'Huyton Gate' until regular timetables were produced. The line was quadrupled, possibly in 1871, with the additional lines to the north. At the junction, about half a mile east of the station, two lines go east to Earlestown with the St Helens' line passing north east to Prescott.

THATTO HEATH. Unlike Prescott, the station buildings are standard LNWR wooden ones. This view of a Wigan bound train also shows the interlocking bricks used for the platforms, the gas lights and the absence of a canopy although there is a room in which to wait for trains. Of interest are the suburban coaches of this postwar train. Being non-corridor, each compartment had a door, operable by letting the window down on a leather strap and then turning the handle from the outside. The station staffs' job was to go and shut all the open doors before the train could proceed – hardly conducive to smart timings.

THATTO HEATH. The train is departing on its way to Wigan. On the Liverpool platform can be seen the small wooden booking office; further along, the platform facilities had a canopy. The railway company believed that more passengers would be waiting here and so provided better protection. Just beyond the over bridge in the Liverpool direction, the single signal post, carrying arms for both directions, was hoisted up in the air for visibility.

PRESCOTT STATION, EXTERIOR, 1907. The station boasted a simple, clean cut set of buildings sporting the latest in passenger protection – a covered footbridge.

PRESCOTT STATION, INTERIOR, 1906. The station opened its doors to passengers for the first time on 1 January 1872; freight trains had been able to use the line two weeks earlier. This view from the adjacent over bridge reveals a not too-densely populated area and two trains passing. The presence of the bridge means that signals would be obscured and so they were put onto tall posts to lift them into the sky-line; the starter signal on the right also has its arm repeated at the normal height for the benefit of trains stopping at the station, as shown.

Six
Garswood to St Helens

Until the mid 1860s, colliery owners around Wigan had but one port for their product: Liverpool, along the L&Y. It was not surprising that they should unite to form the Lancashire Union Railway in an independent attempt to connect up with the LNWR line at St Helens, and the access to Garston's docks. This move was strongly supported by the LNWR. The original plan was for the line, after it had skirted eastern and southern Wigan, to join the line for Widnes to the south of St Helens near Peasley Cross, so avoiding St Helens. While something similar was the final outcome, this wasn't the way the line was built. The line that opened in 1869 joined the existing line north of St Helens, at Gerard's Bridge.

CARR MILL VIADUCT 1905. The original line was widened between Carr Mill Junction and Ince Moss (Wigan), opening in 1892. This necessitated building a duplicate set of piers and iron work to carry the lines over a dip in the landscape and an adjacent lake. This view from the north shows a Wigan bound train passing the junction signal box with Carr Mill station buildings in the rear. The train looks to be an LNWR 4-4-2T hauling a fair length of six wheel coaches.

CARR MILL VIADUCT, 1969. The 2.07 from Wigan to Liverpool, Lime Street, crosses the viaduct on 19 April. In steam days this type of service ran approximately every hour, taking just over the hour to call at all stations. DMUs regularised the service and speeded it up by around fifteen minutes. At the end of the viaduct the train passed Carr Mill Junction. This was where the fast lines continued to St Helens, while the slow lines went south on their way to Sutton Oak, avoiding the passenger station. As the mines became worked out, so the lines were reduced: the quadruple lines by 1964, and the line to Sutton Oak in the very late 1960s.

CARR MILL VIADUCT, 1954. This rail enthusiast's train stopped on the viaduct for photographs and the like. It then continued to Widnes. Notice how the lines are fastened to longitudinal sleepers and the continuous check rails to prevent derailment.

GARSWOOD, 1970. The two main stations along the line, Garswood and Bryn, both had brick buildings on their platforms which are still open today. Although it is over one hundred years since it opened, this view towards St Helens, apart from minor changes, is very similar to the original.

GARSWOOD, c. 1950. So busy was the line, that the LNWR built an additional pair of freight lines in 1882. These by-passed the station to the south and, in the above view, went through the bridge to the left in the background. Sighting problems made necessary these magnificently tall signals with lower repeaters.

HAYDOCK JUNCTION, 1964. The original 1832 Broad Oak branch north from Sutton Oak Junction was extended north to Blackbrook in 1850, and in 1880, even further north, to meet the Wigan to St Helens' line at Carr Mill. This enabled collieries to be connected to the railway system. Traffic was plentiful resulting, by 1862, in the doubling of the lines. To cope with the volume of traffic from the mines, sidings were developed at the Broad Oak branch, at Marsh's, while it was being enlarged in 1858. This line effectively created a St Helens' Station by-pass. Coal trains destined for Widnes and Garston's docks could pass all the way on either practically dedicated lines or lightly used passenger lines. Doing just that in March, was Stanier 8F No. 48318 hauling the Long Meg to Widnes limestone hoppers. Ahead of the train is Fleet Lane signal box followed by Marsh's Sidings. Engines could pass west here to Sutton Oak shed. Not only could trains from the colliery get onto BR lines here, but also at Earlestown and Ashton-in-Makerfield.

MARSH'S SIDINGS. Looking north, the double track line can be seen coming in from Fleet Lane Crossing, Haydock Junction and ultimately, Carr Mill Junction. The sidings were soon to be lifted and the trailing connection to the factory on the up side had seen busier days.

MARSH'S SIDINGS. This time Bold Colliery is on the sky line. The main line curves to the left and will join up with the passenger lines at Sutton Oak Junction, some half a mile south. Curving away to the right is the single line to Broad Oak Junction, skirting Sutton loco shed. Another triangle within this one existed; together they allowed extensive goods and light engine movements without hampering the main lines.

POCKET NOOK JUNCTION. This was to the north and on the other side of the line to No. 1 box. One of the original branches of the line from Peasley Cross Junction went to collieries and industries north of St Helens, for example at Cowley Hill. Much of it was doubled in 1856 and, with the opening of the through station for the Rainford branch in 1858, an effective St Helens' Station avoiding line had been created. From 1 November 1869, this line was improved and later in the year, the LU line from Wigan fed traffic into the area north of St Helens' Station. The part south of the bridge, over the canal by Atlas Foundry, for approximately 350 yards to Hardshaw Brook Chemical Works was single track.. A large number of local industries such as the extensive Sutton Alkali Works, brick works and chemical works, were also served from sidings that came together at this junction. Controlling events was this LNWR thirty-nine lever frame box.

CANAL CROSSING. This shows wonderfully well how the canal and railway co-existed. Lines were simply on a turn bridge that could be swung to allow a barge to pass. The line is from Pocket Nook Junction, off to the left, to Peasley Junction, south of St Helens' Station, so forming a by pass. Just after the group of wagons the line became single for a short distance. This, together with the weight restrictions that were imposed due to the bridges, restricted the usefulness of the line to anything other than short freight trips and small locos.

Seven

Glazebrook to St Helens

The Wigan Junction Railway was developed from Glazebrook, on the CLC main line between Manchester and Liverpool, opening to Strangeways (near Wigan) on 16 October 1879 and, three and a half years later, to passengers on 1 April 1884. Ince was reached in 1884 and Wigan itself, in 1892. A curve to the west of Glazebrook Station allowed through trains between Manchester to Wigan. A west to north curve was put in by the GCR in July 1900, so allowing movements between the Wigan and St Helens' coal fields to Liverpool and the docks. It also permitted Haydock Park race course meeting trains to go west.

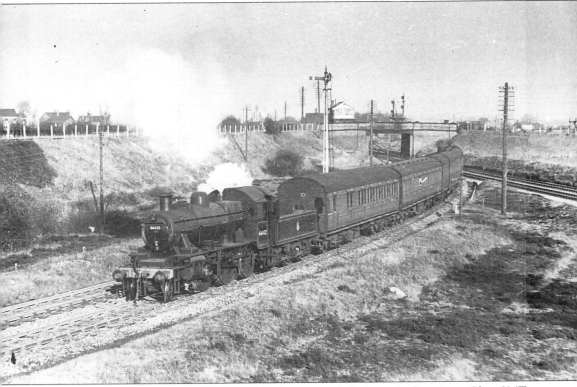

GLAZEBROOK WEST JUNCTION, 1956. Having just left the main line, Ivatt Class 2MT 2-6-0 No. 46432, hauls a train to Wigan Central on 10 March. The single arm posts protect the junction for east bound trains, their height has been dictated by the over bridge. The signal box overseeing events is also hoisted skywards so that signalmen could see their trains and the tail lights of passing trains.

GLAZEBROOK WEST JUNCTION, 1959. The 2.15 from Irlam to Wigan Central leaves Glazebrook on 24 September hauled by Ivatt Class 2MT No. 46448. Showing up above the over bridge are the controlling signals, which now have BR upper quadrant arms. The arms of the main line taller because it is the main route. The top arms are the starters for the station, while the bottom arms are the distants for the boxes in front, namely, Glazebrook Moss Junction and Dam Lane Junction.

GLAZEBROOK, 1959. Looking east from a road bridge, this view shows the Manchester platform and the goods yard in detail. Note the coal being bagged up and loaded onto a lorry. The train consists of chemical wagons, probably bound for Widnes and is hauled by Stanier 8F 2-8-0 No. 48208.

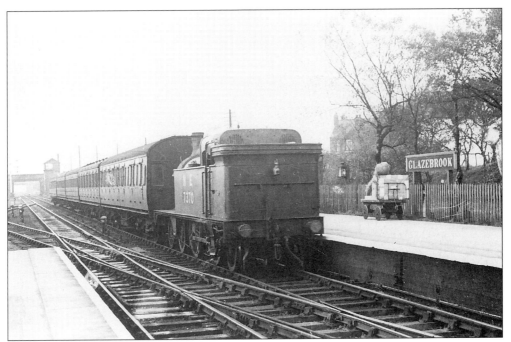

GLAZEBROOK, 1946. Entering from Warrington is LNER Class C13 4-4-2T No. 7370 on 18 October. After picking up passengers that had left St Helens on the 9.35, the train would take twenty-five minutes to serve all the stations to Manchester Central.

GLAZEBROOK. This was one of a series of almost identical stations along the line from Trafford Park (Manchester) and Cressington Junction (Liverpool). This view is from the adjacent over bridge and looks towards Liverpool, with the junction signals standing out on the sky-line. The characteristic station buildings show up well and there was a small shelter on the other platform. Nothing much has changed on the passenger side but the goods yard has closed.

CULCHETH, 1964. On both platforms were wooden shelters but that on the Glazebrook platform was larger and had a canopy; both sides were accessed by ramps from the adjacent over bridge. Standard Class 4MT 4-6-0 No. 75057 is hauling the 2.15 Irlam to Wigan Central on the last day of service, 1 November. Nearby, New Church Halt had platforms made out of sleepers supported on brick piers. Passenger accommodation was provided by a grounded ex-Great Eastern six-wheel coach.

CULCHETH, 1961. A Wigan to Manchester train is being hauled by Stanier 2 cylinder 2-6-4T No. 42465 in March. The station looks neat and tidy: often the case where staff were local residents. In the 1960s Warrington became a New Town with the resulting expansion of population in such areas. Unfortunately, the 'Beeching Axe' arrived in 1964, before the impact of the extra people had been seen.

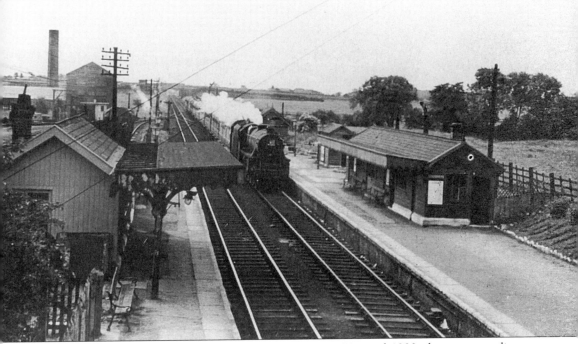

LOWTON. From the opening of the line to Wigan in 1879, until 1900, this was an ordinary country station. It was the opening of the line from the CLC main line at Hunt's Cross to Fazackerley in 1880 and Southport in 1884, that made Wigan and St Helens' people think that a different route to Liverpool's docks and the coast could be achieved. Businessmen were carried away by the amounts of coal that could be mined but financial problems bedevilled the project. The proposed triangle at Lowton became a south to west curve only, and the ten mile extension from St Helens to Fazackerley never materialised. Passing through the station is a train from Glazebrook bound for Haydock racecourse, hauled by an unidentified Black Five', in the 1950s.

LOWTON. This view looks north towards Wigan. When the branch to St Helens opened on 2 January 1900, the wooden station buildings were re-built as a certain amount of passenger transfer would occur, hence the larger than average facilities, including anopies on both platforms. Access was from the adjacent road bridge. What a splendid example of a GCR bracket signal! Its height is to assist visibility with respect to the bridge.

LOWTON ST MARY'S. This rather creased, pre-grouping photograph is typical of Victorian times: whenever a photographer arrived, everybody turned out to pose. The engine is a smartly turned out Great Central 2-4-0T. Sacre designed these Altrincham Tanks were built at Gorton in 1881, and shedded at Ince, Wigan. Number 448 is seen with its Parker chimney; in 1911 it became No. 448B. The station name board makes interesting reading.

LOWTON ST MARY'S, 1961. Visible under the bridge is the divergence of the two parts of the GCR system, north to Wigan and west to St Helens. Hauling a summer Saturday only train from Sheffield to Blackpool is Standard Class 9F 2-10-0 No. 92115. It will pass up to Hindley where connections onto the former Lancashire Union Railway will enable it to by-pass Wigan and emerge onto the main line at Standish. The desire of the Wigan Junction Railway, and later the MS&LR, to have a route to Blackpool will have been achieved, but not via Wigan Central as envisaged.

BETWEEN LOWTON AND GOLBORNE, 1961. The busiest part of this ex-GCR branch to St Helens was the eastern end from Lowton St Mary's to Edge Green and Golborne Colliery Sidings box. This served the branch to Crompton's sidings, off to the right, and Golborne Colliery, bottom left. The latter was worked by propelling in empty wagons, as this 4F 0-6-0 No. 44490 has done in March. Full wagons left the colliery onto the ex-LNWR main line. NCB engines were allowed over the section from here to Ashton-in-Makerfield to enter the extensive Haydock Colliery network.

GOLBOURNE. After leaving Lowton St Mary's the St Helens' line passed over the LNWR main line at the point of these rudimentary, all wooden facilities. After nationalisation, this station became the north station, with the main line becoming the south station.

HAYDOCK PARK, 1960. Although passenger services were withdrawn in 1952, the line was used by trains serving the nearby collieries and the nearby race track. Waiting to take race-goers home are Stanier 2-6-4 Tanks. At Glazebrook, the train on the right, No. 42362, would take the original east curve to Manchester. The Liverpool train, hauled by No. 42183, would take the 1900 GCR curve to the west.

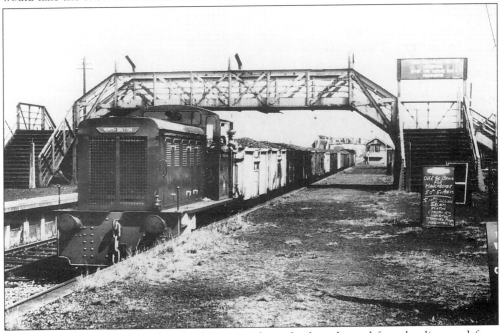

HAYDOCK PARK, 1960. The chief revenue along the line derived from hauling coal from local collieries. Indeed, the line opened to freight traffic on 1 July 1895, almost three and a half years before passengers used it. Here is NCB loco No. 4 passing east with the ubiquitous steel wagons loaded with coal.

ASHTON-IN-MAKERFIELD STATION, EXTERIOR, *c.* 1900. Looking almost like a village school are the station buildings adjacent to the A49 over bridge. The buildings are similar to those at Golbourne.

ASHTON-IN-MAKERFIELD STATION, INTERIOR, *c.* 1910. Although an independent railway, it was run by the MSLR, later the GCR. This view shows an MSLR 2-4-0T hauling an odd assortment of vehicles. The first is a twelve wheel auto coach, probably derived from a steam rail motor train. Next there is a CCT van, then a six wheel, third class coach with a horse box in the rear.

HAYDOCK RACES, 1961. Although the station at Ashton-in-Makerfield closed ten years ago, the goods yard stayed open. After dropping passengers off at the race-course station, some 500 yards in the rear, the coaches would be stabled in the goods yard, to the right. Overnight torrential rain on 2 March flooded the trackbed and was still falling when Stanier 2-6-4T arrived.

HAYDOCK RACES, 1961. A little while later and the same engine is waiting by the twenty-three lever signal box; the patterned barge board is a nice touch. Here it will be given the single line token to enable it to proceed to St Helens' Central.

HAYDOCK STATION, 1952. Passing east to Lowton St Mary's is a freight from St Helens hauled by an unidentified LNER engine. The contrast between the passenger's facilities is noticeable. As few, if any, passengers would wait for trains for the three mile journey to St Helens, there were no buildings on the down platform. Lamps, name board and a small wooden shelter were provided for Lowton and Manchester bound passengers. Access was from the over bridge next to the photographer's position.

ST HELENS' CENTRAL APPROACH, 1952. The prospectus for the line, as quoted by Lord Derby at the cutting of the first sod on 28 January 1888, included the phrase, 'nor any costly viaduct'. Nothing could have been further from the truth. There was one at Golbourne over the LNWR and a 200 yard viaduct had to be built to get the line across the Sankey Canal south, close to the new double locks and the LNWR main line, from its station to Gerard's Bridge. Other branches from the line were to Globe Chemical, Union Plate Glass and collieries in the Pocket Nook area. The line was single from the start of the viaduct to the station yard. Here, at the death throes of the passenger service, LNER J10 0-6-0 No. 65159 goes tender first into Central Station.

ST HELENS' CENTRAL STATION, EXTERIOR, 1 MARCH 1952. Later this day the doors closed for the last time. The brick and tile building is similar in materials to others along the line, such as Ashton and Golbourne. Covered steps at the rear led up to the platform.

ST HELENS' CENTRAL, 1 MARCH 1952. Typical motive power of a J10 and a rake of five non-corridor coaches provide one of the three trains on the last day of passenger service. Just over fifty years before a special train from Manchester arrived for the line's opening to passengers. Sir Henry Seton-Kerr, the town's MP, Lord Newton and the Mayor of St Helens were among the 300 guests at the later banquet.

ST HELENS' CENTRAL, 1951. The passenger facilities were rudimentary: perhaps they were to have been replaced later when the 'Grand Plan was developed to go east to Liverpool and Southport. On the single wooden platform was a small shelter. The seat and the lamp have the station's name on them. With the time just after 9 am of 26 April, J10 loco No. 65159 has arrived at the terminus at the end of an hour's journey, stopping at all the stations from Manchester. It would then detach itself from the coaches, pull forward and using the release facility rein round its coaches. It would then form the 9.35 to Glazebrook.

ST HELENS' CENTRAL LOCO FACILITIES, 1965. This engine had dropped its coaches east along the line and had travelled light to be turned. At the Birchley loco depot there was a two road shed. The turntable was a manual version, the staff held down the brake lever and, using the grips around the well, pushed the engine round: no mean feat for an engine weighing over eighty-seven tons.

ST HELENS' CENTRAL SIGNAL BOX, 1965. This wooden twenty-seven lever signal box was next to Standish Street. The line nearest the box went to the passenger platform while the other line serviced the goods yard, and over the bridge, went to the Pilkington's glass works at Cowley Hill.

ST HELENS' CENTRAL GOODS SHED, 1965. The area between Central and Birchley Streets was an extensive goods yard, complete with engine handling facilities (behind the photographer). The size of the goods shed is in complete contrast to the passenger facilities. The latter had all the trappings of being temporary, while the former were 'in business and here to stay'.

Acknowledgements

This book was born out of the desire to unravel the complex railway network in the heartland of industrial Lancashire. No book is the work of one person and this one is no exception. Its existence is due to persistent research, supported by local people. Without the support of local history libraries and societies in the three major towns, it wouldn't have been possible. I am particularly indebted to residents Graham Earl in Widnes, Dave Forrest in Warrington and Mary Presland in St Helens. I thank them for all their advice, encouragement and help. Special mention must be made of Eddie Bellas, who besides letting me use numerous photographs, provided valuable background information.

Many people have lent me materials and photographs, I hope I have listed them all and apologise in advance for any omissions. As in any historical document, there will be different opinions about the importance and relevance of the evidence. Some data is different depending on the source, therefore, the desire for accuracy continues and if anyone can substantiate or correct a point, I would be only too pleased to hear from them.

Thanks to: R. Humm, N. Preedy, M.A. King, N.D. Mundy, I.G. Holt, H.C. Casserley, J. Peden, J. Mashell, J. Tolson, J. Highcock, A. Appleton, M.H. Walshaw, R.K. Blencowe, P. Hutchinson, G.B. Ellis, L. Hanson, D. Ibbertson, R.S. Carpenter, R. Morten, C. Townley, L. Vaughan, J. Townley, N. Brooksbank, G. Earl, J. Ryan, B. Morrisson, A. Sommerfield, N. Martindale, F. Dean, B. Lord, J. Searson, A. Gilbert, J. Shuttleworth, R. Gee, P. Norton; Stations UK, Pictorail, The Catalyst Museum, G. Coltas, A.K. Jones Collection, British Waterways, R. Humm; Historical Model Railway Society, Lancashire and Yorkshire Railway Society, London and North Western Railway Society, Great Central Railway Society, Signalling Recording Society, Rail and Canal Historical Society, Mowat Collection; Warrington, Widnes and St Helens' Libraries, National Monuments Record Centre.

In today's market place a great number of photographs are for sale: some are copies of originals without the owners knowledge or permission. If, in this book, there is a picture from your collection and I haven't credited you, I apologies.